Embracing Life as a CAT LADY

Lori Vaden, Ph.D.

Archway Publishing books may be ordered through booksellers or by contacting:

Archway Publishing
1663 Liberty Drive
Bloomington, IN 47403
www.archwaypublishing.com
844-669-3957

Because of the dynamic nature of the Internet, any web addresses or links contained in this book may have changed since publication and may no longer be valid. The views expressed in this work are solely those of the author and do not necessarily reflect the views of the publisher, and the publisher hereby disclaims any responsibility for them.

Any people depicted in stock imagery provided by Getty Images are models, and such images are being used for illustrative purposes only.
Certain stock imagery © Getty Images.

ISBN: 978-1-6657-6724-8 (sc)
ISBN: 978-1-6657-6723-1 (hc)
ISBN: 978-1-6657-6725-5 (e)

Library of Congress Control Number: 2024921644

Print information available on the last page.

Archway Publishing rev. date: 12/02/2024

Ailurophile: One who loves cats.

—The American Heritage Dictionary of the English Language, Fifth Edition

To my wonderful husband, who has always supported me. He has always cheered me on and believed in me; I am forever grateful for that.

I also want to dedicate this book to all my friends and fellow animal advocates who share my passion for cats. You know who you are, and I am so grateful for your friendship and support.

I especially want to thank our friend and veterinarian, Dr. Jenny Powers, for her tireless efforts in helping all of our fur babies. Her dedication and compassion are truly inspiring.

Lastly, I wish to dedicate this book to Te, our oldest cat, who passed away. He taught us the true meaning of resilience and courage, and he will always hold a special place in our hearts.

Rest in peace, dear Te. We love you.

In memory of Te (2011–2024).

Acknowledgments

I would like to thank the talented Mei Kei McDowell, of Miss Mei Kei Fine Art and Designs, for my book's cover, certain cat images, photos, and illustrations.

Miss Mei Kei Fine Art and Designs
Website: https://www.missmeikei.com/
Facebook: Miss Mei Kei Fine Art Studio
Instagram: @missmeikei
Email: missmeikeidesigns@gmail.com

I want to express my gratitude to the following individuals for sharing their heartwarming stories and beautiful images for the book. I would like to thank my new friend, Carmen, Grayson's mom; Carole, another new friend, and Sonny's mom; Anne, mother to Kelly Clyde, who helped me find Sonny a home; Carol, my mom and mother to Rusty; Sherry, mom to many, a great friend, and a real cat lady; Gracie, mother to Flower and Tiger; Char, my friend and fellow cat lover, and mother to Beanie and ET; Sandy, Melba's savior; and Mallory, mother to Annie, Abigail, and Mr. Kitty. Thank you all so much!

A Meow from the Author

Welcome, fellow feline enthusiasts and kindred spirits! As you hold this book in your hands, I invite you to join me on a wonderful journey through the world of cat companionship. My name is Lori Vaden, and I proudly wear the badge of a dedicated cat lady. Cats have held a special place in my heart for as long as I can remember. Their independent yet affectionate nature, graceful movements, and mysterious allure have always fascinated me. Through the years, my home has been filled with the comforting presence of purring companions, each with unique personalities and quirks. In this book, I share my personal experiences, adventures, and reflections on embracing a life centered around these captivating creatures.

From the joy of welcoming a new feline friend into your home to the bittersweet moment of saying goodbye, this book delves into the multifaceted world of cat ownership with honesty, humor, and most importantly, love. Whether you are a seasoned cat lady (like me) or a curious soul considering the leap into cat parenthood, this book is not just a source of information but a beacon of inspiration and comfort. Let us celebrate the beauty of embracing life as cat ladies together, one purr at a time. May your days be filled with cozy cuddles, playful antics, and endless love from your furry companions.

With whiskers and warmth,
Dr. Lori Vaden

INTRODUCTION

The term "cat lady" has taken on a negative connotation over the years. Some definitions have referred to a woman who lives alone with several cats and is often viewed as lonely and angry. Historically, women with cats had been considered witches, especially if they had black cats. Some were even thought to be older women who could not have relationships. But the modern cat lady is different.

Being a cat lady today is not necessarily associated with loneliness or being a social outcast; it can reflect a person's love for animals and their choice to share their life with cats. In essence, the modern cat lady is a cat lover who celebrates the joy and companionship that feline friends bring into their lives. They may also actively advocate for animal welfare and adoption. This term has evolved to encompass a diverse range of individuals who proudly embrace their love for cats as a positive aspect of their identities, challenging the negative stereotypes that have been unfairly associated with it.

Over the years, I have gathered a wealth of resources that have not only helped me take care of cats but also deepened my understanding of them. In this book, I share these invaluable tools with you. I also hope you find comfort in the heartwarming stories of my fellow cat-loving friends who, like us, have been touched by the love of cats. If you are a cat lover, I hope you find solace in reading my book and will consider sharing it with others who share our passion for feline friends.

CHAPTER
1

Casual Cat Lover to Cat Lady Extraordinaire

If you were to ask anyone who knows me, they would tell you that I am the quintessential cat lady. I take great pride in being called a cat lady, which signifies my love for all the felines I have helped and cared for. There is nothing that I would not do for them. This book aims to offer you a glimpse into the world of being a cat lover. I share the stories of all the cats—house cats and feral ones—that have come into my life. I also detail my experiences with rescuing cats, living with them, understanding them, and caring for them. Moreover, I showcase the beautiful relationships that I have formed with them.

I did not become a cat lady overnight. It all started when my husband and I moved into our current home over twelve years ago. At that time, we only had dogs. The decision to share my life with multiple cats is rooted in a genuine love for these animals and a desire to provide them with a safe and loving home. I have indoor cats and many outdoor feral cats that I care for daily, each with a unique personality. I take pleasure and solace in their company and distinct personalities. I never expected to have so many, but they have all found their way into my heart, and I would do anything for them.

My husband and I believe in taking care of all animals. Just ask the many raccoons, deer, squirrels, and birds that come to our home! We have had up to five feral cats come to our property at a time. Some cats have stayed around and had kittens, while others have left or passed away. We take pride in building shelters for them to keep warm and dry. You would be amused if you knew how many cat houses, feeding stations, and daily care ideas my husband and I have experimented with over the years. We always aim for perfection but are still learning. I am sure our house is well-known among the feline community for providing the best food and shelter.

I work from home most of the time, and I constantly look outside to see if a cat is hanging around wanting something or checking on all my inside cats. I believe I have gotten pretty good at timing the needs of the cats in my life and attempting to be a real, loving cat lady. I have always been fascinated by them and their mysterious and independent nature. I am also captivated by their playfulness, graceful movements, and the way they exude elegance and mischievousness at the same time. All of them keep me entertained.

Over time, my love for cats has developed into what some may say is a complete obsession, which I have accepted wholeheartedly. As I spent more time with all my cats, I started collecting cat-themed items like books, cups, figurines, and even shirts, filling my living spaces with images and representations of these fascinating creatures. I also get cat-type gifts from my friends.

My bond with my inside and outside feral cats is deeply fulfilling. The joy I feel in having cats is a testament to the unique and rewarding experiences that being a cat lover brings. Perhaps this joy is a way to compensate for not having children, and I am OK with that. I have noticed that I provide my cats with affection similar to a mother's love. Cat ladies like me often dedicate themselves to providing a high quality of life for their feline friends, ensuring they receive proper nutrition, veterinary care, and enrichment. It is also worth noting that many cat lovers are active in animal rescue and advocacy, working to improve the lives of cats in need.

Forming a close relationship with a cat can be a rewarding experience that requires a great deal of trust. I have developed strong emotional bonds with my indoor and outdoor feline companions. Through these close relationships, I have learned to communicate with them uniquely, which involves understanding their different meows, body language, and other subtle signals. While I am still learning, our connections continue to grow stronger.

Being a cat lover can bring joy, companionship, and a sense of purpose. However, it can also come with challenges, such as the responsibility of caring for multiple animals and living with the potential social stigma. It can be expensive due to the costs of food, litter, veterinary care, and other supplies, especially if you have a limited income. Caring for cats can also require significant time, energy, and space, which can be even more challenging if you have many cats.

Exposure to cat dander, fur, or litter can cause health concerns like allergies or asthma. Unfortunately, spending a lot of time with cats can also lead to some isolation, making it difficult to build other relationships and socialize. Finally, cat behavioral problems can arise, particularly if a cat lady has many cats, which can be challenging to manage.

Ultimately, living life as a cat lady means finding fulfillment and happiness through the special bonds shared with feline companions, and embracing the unique joys and responsibilities of being a devoted cat owner. Therefore, it is essential to consider the required commitment of time and energy before deciding to adopt. Fortunately, I am blessed to be able to provide them with the things they need.

CHAPTER
2

Remarkable Cat Ladies and a Few Great Men

Many remarkable women—such as Florence Nightingale, Julia Child, Catherine the Great, Clara Barton, and even Martha Stewart, to name a few—have shared a deep love for their feline companions. These women (and a few great men) I have included have significantly influenced the world through their talents, achievements, and unwavering devotion to their beloved cats. Their love for cats is not just a personal preference but a testament to the unique and special bonds that can be formed with these mysterious and independent creatures.

Florence Nightingale

Believe it or not, Florence Nightingale, the pioneer of modern nursing, was a well-known example of a cat lady. She reportedly owned over sixty cats during her lifetime and took great care of them. Even her nursing attendants are said to have prepared specific meals for each cat. She also believed that cats possess more sympathy and feelings than humans. I would have to agree with her about this. I have met many humans who lack compassion toward animals or others. I do not want to be around anyone like that.

During the Crimean War, Ms. Nightingale believed that cats could provide significant medical benefits by calming soldiers who had been through the trauma of battle. She was reported to have worked tirelessly for months in the war zone, striving to improve the horrendous conditions of the British military. However, the nurses themselves were also subject to appalling conditions, including the constant presence of rats, which was one of the worst situations they faced. However, the situation was helped by the presence of cats.

A house without a cat is like a day without sunshine, a
pie without *fromage*, a dinner without wine.
—Julia Child

Julia Child

Julia Child, a renowned chef who taught us about French cuisine, was also a cat lover. When she and her husband were in Paris, they acquired a cat named Minette Mimosa McWilliams Child. Child immediately fell in love with the feline and even brought Minette with her to the TV shows she hosted.

Catherine the Great

Catherine the Great's fondness for cats is well-documented in historical accounts and letters. She is said to have owned many cats, which not only were her companions but also provided her with comfort and solace during times of stress and solitude. These cats were treated with the utmost care and affection, reflecting Catherine's compassionate nature and love for animals. In addition to being beloved pets, Catherine's cats played a symbolic role in her court.

In Russian folklore, cats were seen as mysterious and enigmatic creatures associated with luck, protection, and wisdom. By surrounding herself with cats, Catherine may have sought to align herself with these qualities, projecting an image of strength, cunning, and grace. One famous anecdote recounts how Catherine the Great once issued an order to have a guard posted at the door of her study to prevent her cats from disturbing her during important meetings and discussions. This story highlights the special place cats held in Catherine's heart and the lengths she would go to ensure their well-being.

Catherine's love for cats extended beyond her own personal collection. She is known to have established a special area in the Winter Palace in Saint Petersburg known as the "Cat Room," where stray cats were taken in, cared for, and allowed to roam freely. This gesture of kindness toward these animals reflects Catherine's compassion and sense of responsibility toward all living creatures, regardless of their status or background.

Catherine the Great's relationship with cats offers us a glimpse into the private life of this remarkable historical figure. Her affection for these animals reveals a softer, more humane side to a ruler known for her political acumen and strategic prowess. By cherishing her feline companions, Catherine demonstrated her love for animals and her capacity for empathy and compassion, qualities that endeared her to many during her reign and continue to inspire admiration to this day.

Clara Barton

Clara Barton, the founder of the American Red Cross, was a cat lover. Her affection for felines is evident in a painting of her cat, Tommy, which hangs in the dining room of her former home in Glen Echo, Maryland—now the Clara Barton National Historic Site. Clara adored all animals, particularly cats. During the Civil War, she was given a kitten with a bow around its neck as a token of appreciation for her work during the Battle of Antietam.

Martha Stewart

Martha Stewart's love for all animals is well-known, and she has showcased her love for them on her TV shows. From helping chicks to caring for cows, she has assisted them all. However, I was surprised to learn that she is a proud owner of many cats. In a 2020 article on Martha Stewart's website, I stumbled upon a story about the names of her pets. The article featured all her cats, from Chiggi to Bartok. Chiggi was Stewart's first cat, and she adopted her from a shelter. Bartok was named after a famous composer. Over the years, Stewart has reportedly owned different types of cats, such as Himalayans, Persians, and even a black cat.

Abraham Lincoln

According to the National Archives, during the nineteenth and early twentieth centuries, cats were occasional pets of many US presidents. Their primary purpose was to control the mouse population in the White House. However, it was not until Abraham Lincoln's presidency that a cat was officially recognized as a pet at 1600 Pennsylvania Avenue.

The Lincolns left their dog, Fido, in Springfield, Illinois, when they moved to Washington. In August 1861, Secretary of State William Seward gave them two cats, Tabby and Dixie. Abraham Lincoln was known to enjoy the company of animals.

Rutherford B. Hayes

In 1878, according to the White House Historical Association, David Sickels, the American consul in Bangkok, Thailand, gifted a female Siamese cat to First Lady Lucy Hayes. The cat, Siam, was intended to be a pet for Hayes's daughter, Fanny. Siam was the first Siamese cat to arrive in the United States when she came in 1879. However, the cat became ill just nine months after her arrival. Despite the president's personal physician's efforts to nurse her back to health with fish, chicken, duck, cream, and oysters, she passed away at the White House. According to additional records, the president sent her remains to the Department of Agriculture to be preserved by a taxidermist.

Theodore Roosevelt

According to the White House Historical Association, Theodore Roosevelt and his family shared the White House with various pets. One of their pets was a six-toed tabby cat named Slippers. This type of cat is known as a polydactyl, which comes from the Greek word meaning "many fingers." Polydactyl cats are known for their excellent climbing and hunting skills.

At the time, a journalist named Jacob Riis shared a funny story about Slippers. At a diplomatic corps dinner on January 11, 1906, President Roosevelt escorted the wife of the Hungarian ambassador, Baroness Hengenmuller, through the Cross Hall from the East Room to the State Dining Room. However, Slippers had decided to nap on the Cross Hall's comfortable carpet. Roosevelt walked around his feline friend and let her continue to sleep.

Calvin Coolidge

According to the National Archives, Calvin Coolidge's cat, Tige, disappeared from the White House in March 1924. The news of his disappearance was reported in the press, and radio stations in Washington broadcast the information to seek help from the public in finding the president's lost cat. Fortunately, Tige was found safe and sound in a navy building half a mile from the Executive Mansion. He was then returned to the White House.

> If man could be crossed with the cat, it would improve
> man, but it would deteriorate the cat.
> —Mark Twain

Mark Twain

Mark Twain was a cat lover and was said to have owned up to nineteen cats. His cats had exciting names such as Apollinaris, Beelzebub, Blatherskite, Buffalo Bill, Satan, Sin, Sour Mash, Tammany, Zoroaster, Soapy Sal, and Pestilence. Twain even included cats in his writings, with the animals appearing in some of his most famous works. A cat named Peter is featured in *The Adventures of Tom Sawyer*, but he is just one of many cats that appear in Twain's works.

Ernest Hemingway

Little did I know until I started researching great cat men that Ernest Hemingway's home, even today, is full of many cats—and not just cats, but polydactyl cats. Nearly sixty of these cats are reportedly present today, and they are most likely descendants of Hemingway's first cat, Snow White, who was also a polydactyl cat. Hemingway was known to have named his cats after famous people like Marilyn Monroe and Harry Truman.

Edwin Hubble

Astronomer and scientist Edwin Hubble made significant contributions to the study of space through his work at the Mount Wilson Observatory in California. In 1946, Hubble and his wife Grace adopted a furry black cat they named Nicolas Copernicus. Hubble grew fond of the cat, which appears in many of his photographs. Reportedly, when Edwin Hubble passed away in 1953, Nicolas Copernicus curled beside him on the bed. For months after Hubble's death, the cat would sit in the window waiting for Hubble to come home.

> There are no ordinary cats.
> —Leonardo da Vinci

Leonardo da Vinci

Leonardo da Vinci, a renowned artist and extraordinary engineer, is widely celebrated for his masterful paintings, such as the *Mona Lisa* and the *Last Supper*. Additionally, he is often credited with inventing groundbreaking technologies, including the tank, helicopter, and parachute. Surprisingly, it is lesser known that he was also fond of painting cats. According to historical records, he may have even started a painting titled *Madonna and Child with Cat*. However, there is no concrete proof that this ever happened.

CHAPTER
3

The Quirky World of Cat Ladies

People who have a strong affection for cats often share similar characteristics. These include being emotional, affectionate, independent, and a little quirky. A cat lover's home is not just a shelter but a kingdom for their feline overlords, and a place to express the essence of being a cat lover. Cat lovers enjoy showing off—and I do as well, especially with my cat-loving friends, who understand my quirkiness and the cat-lover lifestyle.

Despite the negative connotations that the term "cat lady" has often carried, I reclaim and celebrate this label as a badge of honor within my cat-lover community of friends. We all embrace our love for cats, recognizing the joy, companionship, and fulfillment these animals bring to our lives.

Our shared passion and understanding bring us together as cat lovers. We enjoy discussing the latest cat memes, sharing heartwarming stories about our feline friends, and making personal connections. Additionally, we discuss advocacy for feline welfare and responsible pet ownership. We often unite to support local shelters, rescue organizations, and initiatives aimed at improving the lives of needy cats. Our love for all things cat-related creates a sense of connection that transcends age, background, or location.

Whether we are celebrating the joy of welcoming a new cat into our family or comforting each other during difficult times like loss or illness, our cat-lover community serves as a source of strength and understanding. Everyone can find comfort in knowing they are never alone in their journeys as cat lovers, thanks to shared experiences and mutual care.

To share the excitement of being a cat lover, there are many ways to celebrate. Did you know that there is a National Cat Lady Day? Yes, it is true! I thought I knew all there was to know about cats. This particular day is celebrated on April 19 every year. Susan Michals, an author, entrepreneur, and cat lover, created it. She also founded the CatCon convention, an expo and symposium that engages, educates, and entertains thousands of cat lovers worldwide. The convention features the latest products and ideas for cats and their people. So, if you are a cat enthusiast, mark your cat calendar for National Cat Lady Day!

Regarding the calendar, there are so many important cat lady holidays to remember. I have compiled a list of some essential cat lady calendar days that you should not forget. It is important for all cat owners to stay informed about events related to their feline companions, but personally, I believe our cats should be celebrated every day. So mark your calendars ... right meow!

Cat Lady Calendar

🐾 **January 22** is Answer Your Cat's Questions Day. Although an unofficial holiday (and cats, of course, can't speak), this is still a day for cat owners to take some time to answer their cats' questions and deepen the bond between you and your feline friend.

🐾 **February 20** is Love Your Pet Day. This day is not limited to cats but is for all pets. It encourages pet owners to show their pets some extra love and affection. They can be given a special treat, taken out for a walk, or just spend some quality time with them.

🐾 **March 28** is Respect Your Cat Day. On this day, cat owners are encouraged to show their respect for their feline friends by providing a comfortable living space, nutritious food, and plenty of playtime.

🐾 **April 11** is National Pet Day. This is a special day to celebrate all pets and raise awareness about their importance in our lives.

🐾 **April 19** is National Cat Lady Day. This day celebrates the unique bond between women and their cats, appreciating the love and companionship that cats bring to our lives.

🐾 **May 3** is Hug Your Cat Day. On this day, take some time to give your cat a warm and cozy hug as a way to show your affection and bond with your pet.

🐾 **June 4** is Hug Your Cat Day. (Happens twice a year!) As the name suggests, this day is all about giving your cat lots of hugs.

🐾 **July 10** is Kitten Day, a celebration of all things kitten. Whether you have a kitten or simply love them, it's a great chance to share pictures, stories, and facts about these adorable creatures.

🐾 **August 8** is International Cat Day. This day is celebrated worldwide to raise awareness about the importance of cats in our lives. You can celebrate by volunteering at an animal shelter, donating to a cat rescue, or spending some quality time with your feline friend.

🐾 **September 1** is Ginger Cat Appreciation Day. This day is dedicated to ginger cats. It is a great opportunity to celebrate and appreciate these beautiful cats.

- **October 29** is National Cat Day. This day is all about celebrating cats and their importance in our lives.

- **November 17** is National Black Cat Day. This day is dedicated to black cats and their beauty, who are often associated with bad luck and superstition.

- **December 15** is Cat Herders Day. This day celebrates the unique, and sometimes challenging, relationship between cats and their owners. It's a day to celebrate all the things cats bring to our lives, even when they are being a little challenging.

Purrfect Cat Lady Couture

We cat lovers not only need to know when and where to celebrate our beloved felines, but we also have to think about what to wear, cat-themed home decor, and all the fun and quirky accessories. Cat lovers truly have a unique style that celebrates their special bonds with their furry friends. Whether you consider yourself a dedicated cat lover or appreciate the charm of cat-themed items, the cat-lover style is all about celebrating our wonderful connections with our beloved feline companions.

I have a collection of cat-themed items that I have acquired over the years. Some were purchased, while others were given to me as gifts by friends during events or holidays. I have a variety of cat-themed accessories such as bracelets, earrings, and necklaces, as well as bags with cat faces or ears, scarves, and hats with "Cat Lady" written on them. I also have plenty of cat-themed household items like coffee cups, pictures, and books about cats. Although I do not wear a lot of cat-themed clothing, I enjoy collecting these items and showing them off to my fellow cat-loving friends.

CHAPTER
4
My Feline Family

Embracing life as a cat lady has been the best thing that has ever happened to me. I never knew I would be as in love with my feline family as I am now. Although I may have saved them from being alone and hungry, they have given me much more, and I am proud to share their stories and beauty with you.

Our feline family includes six cats: Leeloo, Lana, Jack, Maybelline, Scotty, and our very new addition, Daisy, who just barely made it in the cover photo. They are all rescues with unique personalities, bringing immense joy and love into our lives. My felines and my two dogs, Suki and Sally, also known as Soup and Salad, are like my children. Sometimes, I find myself rocking my cats to sleep on my lap, washing the gunk out of their eyes, talking to them softly, asking them if they are OK, and even carrying them around the house on my shoulder—not the dogs, though! If you are a cat lover, you understand. You may have done the same thing. I always seem to know when they need affection or someone to hold them; it comes naturally to me now.

Over the years, I have become very indulgent with our cats. I give them everything they desire, maybe too much. I feel this way because all of them have been rescued from difficult situations, and I want to make sure they live happy, comfortable lives.

My husband and I are grateful for their presence every day. Unfortunately, after starting this book, our oldest cat, Te, passed away. He was fourteen years old and had feline immu-nodeficiency virus (FIV), which ultimately took his life. You will learn all about him and caring for an FIV-positive cat, and how Te lived a long and wonderful life despite the disease. I hope that you enjoy learning about all of our wonderful felines.

The smallest feline is a masterpiece.
—Leonardo da Vinci

Te: Tough Enough

Te, our beloved older feline, was affectionately known as Tough Enough. He was a domestic short-haired gray cat with the most memorable eyes. Whenever he saw something he wanted, his eyes would widen with curiosity and intent. His pupils would get so big that his eyes appeared almost black. When he was in a good mood or wanted attention, he would stare at you with an endearing expression. He was such a handsome boy!

Te's long, thin tail had a unique movement: when he was irritated, he would snap the end of it like a rattlesnake. He was quite thin but made up for it with his razor-sharp claws, which felt like tiny needles. He would use them to gently tap on your leg as he waited for you to give him what he wanted.

His story is one of survival and miracles. He was a stray cat who had been thrown out of a car and left with a broken jaw, a hurt nose, as well as other bumps and bruises. He also had feline immunodeficiency virus (FIV), a common virus that attacks the immune system in cats. He was about a year old when he found us and needed a loving home. One day, as my husband was leaving his business, he noticed a skinny, gray cat with its paw reaching through the side of the fence just outside the door. It was dark outside and raining, but he heard the cat's meow and knew he needed help. My husband called me, and we immediately took the cat to the emergency vet.

Despite his health challenges, Te proved to be "tough enough" and brought joy to our whole family. Evidently, he was brilliant and used this to compensate for his lack of good health and strength. He had a unique talent for opening doors, especially those with push-down handles. We called him Houdini. He used his left paw to press down on the door handle, hang on to it, and shift his weight back until the door opened. One time, he opened the door to the garage and let all the other cats out, which set off the home alarm and caused a bit of a scare and chaos. The police responded, and when my husband and I got home shortly after, we were surprised to see that all the cats were in the garage.

Te was a delightful cat with a mischievous streak. He loved to sneak up on you if you were in a room and would peek around the corner and want you to put your hand on the door frame so he could attack you. However, despite this, he was a lovable feline who enjoyed kneading his blanket and observing the world from his kitty pod. Whenever I cooked in the kitchen, Te liked to hang out with me, especially when I cooked bacon or anything with meat and cheese. If I made something sweet that I knew he could eat, I'd let him lick the bowl, like a child would, and he loved the attention.

Te was also a unique cat and had a special bond with our dogs. He had picked up some of their habits, such as running outside to greet us whenever we returned home. Sometimes, he would even jump into the back of the car after we went shopping, curious to see what we had brought back. Seeing him put his head inside the bags, his eyes filled with anticipation, was always delightful. And we never disappointed him; there was always something special about Te, and we would always spoil him.

Although it has been difficult for our family to cope with Te's death, we find comfort in the belief that he is now playing with other cats in a better place, free from FIV. At first, the only image I could see when I thought about him was of his eyes looking up at me from the carrier as I sat in the back seat with him in front of the veterinarian, waiting to say goodbye. That image haunted me for a few weeks, and I made it a point not to remember him like that, and instead, to remember him for what he really was: a strong soul!

Although his health deteriorated rapidly in the month leading up to his passing, he fought with all his might for almost fourteen years, and I feel grateful to have had him in my life. Our whole family feels honored to have been able to share our lives with him.

I have learned a lot about cats through caring for Te. There are many things that felines can catch during their lives, and the majority of them can be prevented by vaccinations, but there is no vaccination for FIV. Because of Te's FIV, I thought it appropriate to share what it is really like to live with and care for an FIV-positive cat. Living with an FIV-positive cat in a multicat household with proper management to ensure the health and well-being of all cats is absolutely possible. If you are managing a multicat household with one FIV-positive cat, some important considerations and tips can help you ensure the health and safety of all your cats. These tips are based on my experience with Te.

Regular checkups with a veterinarian are essential to monitor the cat's health and manage any potential issues that may arise from the virus. Te would go into what my vet described as a kind of remission, where he would gain weight, eat well, etc., but it would not last long, and his body would go back the other way.

FIV-positive cats should be kept indoors to reduce the risk of exposure to other cats and infections. This helps prevent the spread of the virus to other cats and reduces the cat's risk of contracting secondary infections. All of my house cats live indoors only. My husband and

I try to take all of them outside for a few minutes once or twice a month, but we always watch what they are doing and what they are getting into to ensure they do not get sick.

A balanced diet is essential for maintaining the cat's overall health and immune system. Of course, with Te, we fed him by hand for a long time until his injuries were better than when we'd first found him. I remember the emergency vet telling us that he would not live very long, but he lived for fourteen years because we did everything we could to improve his life.

Stress can also weaken the immune system, so it is important to provide a calm and stress-free environment for your cat. Ensure your cat has a quiet place to retreat to, and plenty of opportunities for mental and physical stimulation. Keeping your cat active and engaged can help boost their immune system and overall well-being.

It is important to watch for changes in your cat's behavior, appetite, or litter box habits. My husband and I were always looking for changes in Te's appetite and making sure his stomach and litter box visits were healthy.

Depending on a cat's health status, your veterinarian may recommend certain medications or treatments to manage symptoms or prevent secondary infections. Over the years, Te had to take many medicines, some to give him energy, others to keep him from throwing up his food, and even some for a healthy gut.

Regular testing for secondary infections, such as dental or upper respiratory infections, is essential for maintaining your cat's health. We would get Te regular blood tests to monitor his immune function. He would also get his teeth cleaned yearly, and there were times when we had to have some teeth extracted because his body could not absorb the nutrients needed to keep his teeth healthy.

FIV-positive cats require the same love, attention, and affection as any other cat. It is important to spend quality time with them, provide a comfortable living environment, and ensure they feel safe and secure. With proper care and management, many FIV-positive cats can live long, happy lives like Te did!

Leeloo

Leeloo, also known as Gray Cloud, is our second rescue. When she enters a room, everyone scatters! Leeloo came into our lives and became part of the family when she was just a four-week-old kitten. She was so small that I could carry her in my hand. The day we got her, I put her on my shoulder while my husband and I shopped at PetSmart for all the cute kitten stuff she needed.

Leeloo, a Russian Blue, is a unique-looking cat weighing over fourteen pounds. She meows loudly if you talk too loudly, and she loves to knead and spit on you. She was introduced to Te and our dog Boot that we had at the time, and she fit right in. Te took Leeloo under his paw when she arrived, and it was heartwarming despite his health problems. He would wrap his paws around her so she would not move while he washed her as if she were really dirty. It was strange since he was a male, and she was a female. But he seemed so happy to have her in the house as a companion. Te and Leeloo remained close until he passed.

Russian Blue cats are an elegant breed. They are known for their beauty and gentle nature. They have a silver-blue, plush, and soft coat and bright-green eyes. They are also very intelligent, observant, and sensitive to their owners' moods. Maybe that is why Leeloo gets a bit nervous when anyone talks loudly. If she hears voices that are louder than usual, or if she hears you singing, she will start talking (a.k.a. meowing) repeatedly until she is recognized. She is saying, "Please keep it down; I am trying to nap."

Leeloo was named after a character in a movie that my husband and I watched. If you have seen the movie *The Fifth Element*, released in 1997, you might remember Leeloo, who represented the "cosmic weapon" actor Bruce Willis was searching for. We thought that would be an excellent name for our kitten, and it suited her perfectly. As she grew more significant, she got the name Gray Cloud because everyone got out of her way when she moved around the house. Even though she is a lovebug, some of the other cats and the dogs tiptoe around her, perhaps because of her size.

Leeloo is a sweet cat, but she can be mischievous when she wants to be. My husband and I rescued another cat we named Maybelline, whom you will hear about later, and she and Leeloo do not quite get along well. They tolerate each other and can eat in peace, but sometimes, I catch Leeloo peeking around a corner, looking at Maybelline, and she is ready to chase her when she comes around the corner. At first, this was a bit funny, but after a while, I knew Leeloo was not playing; she was stalking Maybelline. I started correcting her behavior, hoping she would not do it again.

Lana

When a winter ice storm hit our area, a tiny kitten appeared on our front porch. The kitten huddled near the door as if begging to come inside, as if it had been lost and had finally come home. As we watched it roll around, we knew it belonged inside. My husband ventured outside, and although the kitten ran to our neighbor's yard, he was able to catch up with it. We brought it inside to provide it with some much-needed warmth, food, and overall help—and we found out it was a female. We named her Lana.

Like Leeloo, we named Lana after one of the characters in a show we loved to watch called *Archer*. There was a character named Lana, and she had such huge hands. Our kitten, Lana, had really big paws, so we knew Lana would be her name.

Getting Lana to the veterinarian was a priority. She was extremely sick and could hardly breathe. Her eyes were watery and seemed like they were closed because of all the stuff in them. When we got Lana to the vet, she was diagnosed with an upper respiratory infection. We also learned that those big paws were not just big paws but something different.

The veterinarian determined that she had six toes on each front paw. A cat born with six toes is considered to be a polydactyl cat. According to veterinarians, the condition that causes a cat to have extra toes is caused by a genetic mutation.

Lana really had a hard time walking, and we discussed the possibility of surgery. Lana eventually had to receive surgery to have the extra toes removed, and she made a full recovery. However, she had her paws bandaged, and when she tried to use the litter box, it was so hard to watch. We would have to guide her and also cover things up for her. We also had to keep her away from Te and Leeloo so she could heal properly. My husband and I used to refer to the guest room upstairs where Lana was kept for a few weeks as the "cat hospital."

Lana is a stunning cat with soft fur and impressive muscles. We once joked that she might be related to a bobcat, based on her build and strength, but she is a tabby cat with beautiful markings. Her fur is as soft as that of a rabbit, and she is considered a mother cat and a peacemaker in our house. She is the only one of our indoor cats who readily accepts new feline additions to our home. She shows them affection, and they all look up to her. None of the other cats that have graced our house have tried to pick a fight with her. She is a very special cat; we feel lucky to have saved her life. You will learn more about her motherly love and affection when reading about our cat Scotty.

Jack

Before I talk to you about Jack, I need to let you know that our dog, Boot, passed away in 2013. My husband and I were very saddened by his loss. Boot was almost fourteen years old. He was a rescue Rhodesian Ridgeback and a loyal companion. Losing him was especially difficult for me, since I had adopted him from a no-kill shelter when he had been just under a month old. He had been there for me through many challenging times in my life, so his loss was deeply felt.

Not too long after Boot passed away, something miraculous happened. Jack, a black, short-haired cat with beautiful eyes, started to appear on our front porch. He would rub against me, seeking love and attention. One day, as I was sitting in a chair at the back of the house, Jack came up to me and sat on my lap, resting his head on my leg. I felt an instant connection with him, as I had the first time I'd seen Boot. Boot was speaking to me through him. Maybe because I was so hurt from the loss. That day was indescribable. I knew it was Boot sending me love through Jack, and I could feel it.

I love all of my cats, both house cats and feral cats, but Jack is very special to me because of that day. He has been like the child I could never have. He lets me carry him around the house on my shoulder as he collapses his head and stretches his front legs out as if comfortable and content.

A few years ago, when commuting to a job and having a place to stay near my work for the week, I would bring Jack and Leeloo so they could be with me during the week. I would go to bed around 10:00 p.m., and Jack got used to that; so, every night around 10:00 p.m., he would start meowing and head straight to the bedroom. He still continues to stick by his bedtime. Every night, he sleeps above my head on the pillow. He follows me around the house. And if I leave, my husband says he meows and walks around as if he is searching for me. I call him Little Man because he is my excellent companion, and I love him dearly.

Jack is also very handsome. He is a black cat with little gray hairs coming from his ears and a small patch of gray on his chest. He has gorgeous eyes that seem to look right through you. I crave his affection sometimes, and he is always there for me. I love cuddling up with him and talking to him. Because of our close relationship, Jack is very jealous of the other cats—and even sometimes of my husband. The joke in our house is that I created a monster.

Jack will throw a fit if my husband and I are near each other, or if I am loving on another cat in the house. His fits include meowing, running around the house, getting on his side and circling around a carpet with his claws, and even scratching the furniture ... but I love him very much.

I had never had a completely black cat before, and I was very intrigued with how handsome he was. Black cats often get a bad reputation around Halloween, as they are associated with witches and other spooky things. However, this is not a belief shared across the world. A black cat is a sign of good luck in countries like England, Japan, Ireland, and Scotland. In ancient Egypt, cats were even worshiped as embodiments of the gods.

Interestingly, according to the American Society for the Prevention of Cruelty to Animals (ASPCA), there are more black cats than any other color. This is because the genes causing black coloration in cats are the most dominant. Due to their sheer numbers, black cats often receive additional promotion and attention in shelters nationwide because they are less likely to be adopted, and in some cases, people even harm them. Which is horrible to think about.

National Black Cat Day aims to eliminate this stigma by celebrating black cats as cute, lovable, and furry friends. I have never thought that our sweet Jack brought any luck other than good for me and my family.

Maybelline

Maybelline is also a tabby cat with a gorgeous coat, like Lana. The colors of her coat create a dramatic swirling pattern that is easy to identify. Maybelline and Lana have the same fur patterns, but Maybelline's fur is a bit lighter than Lana's. Oh, and her eyes are gorgeous. I remember the first time they looked up into mine on the day we found her.

She was so tiny and vulnerable, and her cry for help pierced my heart. I needed to take care of her. One of my neighbors had discovered Maybelline inside an old, nonfunctioning groundwater meter that did not have a top. At the time, she was just a few weeks old, her eyes were barely open, and she had underdeveloped ears. She had been meowing and whimpering, most likely looking for her mother. I took her in, fed her with a bottle, and made her a part of our family. It was the first kitten I had ever had to bottle-feed because she had no mother. That was a real learning experience for me, as I would get up in the middle of the night to feed her at specific times, and I'd make sure she was using the litter box. I treated her just like a baby.

Thanks to Lana's motherly instinct, Maybelline was socialized and was quickly introduced to the rest of the family. I had Maybelline in my home office upstairs, with a gate across the door so she could not get out but could still see the other cats and what was happening. All the cats would go up to the gate to peek in and get a glimpse of the little thing bouncing around in front of the gate. Leeloo and Te would not stay too long, but long enough to give Maybelline the glimpse that would tell her who was boss around the house. Our dog, Suki, and our cat, Lana, were the ones who really made Maybelline feel welcome and at home. They would lay down in front of the gate and nudge at it, trying to get Maybelline to play. However, Maybelline started looking for ways to get past the gate so she could really play, including climbing over it. And she was successful.

Despite being spayed and never having kittens of her own, Lana had a loving heart and took Maybelline under her wing after she was able to roam the house. Lana basically showed her the ropes. Maybelline took to the litter box, played with all the other cats, and ate well. I was surprised because she was a feral kitten. Maybelline is now known as Daddy's Girl. She is more affectionate and responsive to my husband, even though I rescued her and bottle-fed her.

At some point, Maybelline began having difficulty getting along with some of the other cats. Leeloo and Jack would always bully her and chase her. We consulted with our veterinarian and discovered that Maybelline might have been experiencing stress as a result. Consequently, we decided to put her on medication to help alleviate her stress. I closely observed their interactions and tried to figure out what was wrong. My hunch was that it could be territorial behavior or a health issue. I tried everything I could think of to resolve the conflicts between them. I experimented with pheromone-releasing plug-ins, medications, and immediate corrective actions. However, Jack, although he is my Little Man, has been one of the main troublemakers bothering her. He can be a little mean at times.

Scotty

Scotty is also a black cat, like Jack, but with longer hair and a much bigger body. Let's put it this way: he will resemble a panther if he grows bigger. He has played a crucial role in helping my husband and me understand the significance of trapping, neutering, and releasing cats. Although we had provided food and shelter to feral cats for several years, we had not fully realized the value of spaying and neutering until Scotty came into our lives. We knew very little about the organizations that worked toward this cause.

One day, a mother cat with her four little kittens appeared in our backyard, and I was concerned about their survival as I had seen many come and go over the years. I wanted to make sure these guys survived and got a good home. So I contacted a local organization that spays and neuters felines (trap-neuter-return, or TNR). Together, we planned to trap the mother and kittens, which was a success. I even helped trap two of the kittens myself, which made me appreciate the process more.

My plan was to foster the kittens until we found them a new home. I set up four kennels on top of folding tables, each with food, bedding, and a small litter box inside. After capturing the kittens, we put them in the kennels. The mother was trapped, spayed, and released back in our yard, too, but she did not stay around. I assumed this was because we had taken the kittens.

The kittens adapted very well and were getting used to me coming and going to care for them all day. I noticed that all the kittens would hide behind the only black one in the bunch, as if it were their protector. I saw something extraordinary in that kitten.

At first, I had thought there were two females and two males, but to my surprise, they were all males. One by one, they were adopted, but I had already decided to adopt the black one and had named him Scotty; he was incredibly handsome. It took some time to socialize him since he was skittish, but that was because he was a feral cat. I thank God that I could socialize him enough that he was comfortable with our other five cats. Now, he is part of the family and runs around. He enjoys the company of the other cats, and it is a special moment when he comes up to you and meows, wanting you to pet him or pick him up. I put him on my shoulder, similar to what I do with Jack, and he relaxes his whole body, allowing me to rub him a little. However, as he gets older, he is a bit more independent and only lets me hold him when it is on his terms.

Scotty is a special boy, but I have not mentioned that Lana took Scotty under her wing when he arrived. After adopting Scotty, I brought him into our Carolina room, which can be closed off, but the other animals can see in, and Scotty could see outside into the backyard. We first put him in a pet playpen so he would not hurt himself. The only cat that we would let inside the Carolina room with him was Lana.

No matter whether another cat or kitten is female or male, Lana seems to go into automatic mommy mode to make sure they are taken care of. She really knows no adversaries, only friends. Sometimes, Lana shows the other cats the same thing we showed her: that everything will be all right and we will take care of them. Scotty certainly received that information when he arrived. Now, he is sad when Lana is just in the other room.

Daisy

Daisy is a female gray-and-white tabby cat who recently showed up in our yard. She was about six months old and in great health. I first noticed her sitting on one of our benches on the front porch, grooming herself and having some treats. I started leaving food and water for her, and she began to come around every day.

I first called her Sneaky, because she sneaked around the yard, but I soon grew concerned about her well-being. After discussing it with my husband, we decided to take her in. When she appeared in the backyard, I let her in, and we prepared a comfortable area for her with all the supplies she needed. We named her Daisy! And, as you can see, she is beautiful!

Daisy was initially a bit timid being indoors after having spent so much time outside, but she surprised us by being very sociable and affectionate. She also quickly learned how to use the litter box, and we were amazed by how smart she was. The next day, I called our veterinarian and was pleasantly surprised to get an appointment on the same day.

The vet confirmed that Daisy was in great health, vaccinated her, and scheduled her for spaying. Daisy is adjusting well, and has become one of the family. She is a lot like Te because of the different things she does. We could not be happier to have her with us.

If My Cats Could Talk

If my cats could talk, I might be a bit scared! And people would definitely call me a crazy cat lady! I think, if they could talk, they would all ask why I've put so many pictures of them in this book. I find my cats to be incredibly beautiful and handsome, and it is hard to do them justice with words alone, especially when they strike new poses and make different expressions every day that make me want to take more pictures of them.

I communicate with my indoor and feral cats daily. I speak to them softly, asking them how they are doing, complimenting their beauty or handsomeness, and expressing gratitude for having them in my life, even if only for a short time. Sometimes, they tilt their heads to the side in an attempt to understand what I am saying. If the cats in my life could talk, they would have a lot to share.

Te always talked a lot. He would meow right in your face for something. If he could really talk, he would have asked us why he could not be the only cat in the house, and why we had to keep growing the family. He might also have asked why we changed the doorknob on the garage door, even though he knew he was a magician at opening it.

I believe that Te would have also thanked my husband and me for saving his life, never giving up on him, giving him all the cream cheese his heart desired, letting him go outside with the dogs every time the door opened, giving him food from our plates, and dealing with him trying to steal our food. Finally, I believe that now, from kitty heaven, he would remind us that, although he fought hard through a lot and had lots of health problems, he is grateful for all that we did for him and that we do not cry because he is free of pain and filled with happiness.

Jack already talks too much, if you ask me, but if he could really tell me something, it would be that he belongs to me, and nobody else is allowed on my lap or the bed, or even near me. He would also ask if we could get our own place! I believe he would also tell me that he does not like Leeloo or Maybelline, and that Scotty is pushing it by following him around the house. I know this is true because I have seen Scotty, who is still like a kitten despite his size, following Jack around the house, not to hurt him, but to play. But Jack is older and set in his ways, so he initially ignores Scotty, but they are prone to occasional sparring.

If Lana could talk, she would ask for more treats and tell me that she enjoys mothering all the other cats in the house. If Leeloo could talk, she would have a sock or toy in her mouth at the same time while she begged to sit on your chest and knead you. She might also ask to go outside and sit in the sunshine.

If Scotty could talk, I think he would say, "Where's my mama?" That means he wants Lana. But, seriously, I think he would also say he thanks us for adopting him. He might even ask if all three of his brothers had received good homes, and if Lana is his real mommy. Although she is not, she provides him with so much love and affection. He might also ask why we have to put a collar on him. He runs when he hears the bell on the collar, but we always catch him when he wants treats, so we can put it on him.

If Maybelline could talk, she would tell Leeloo and Jack to piss off! They pick on her too much sometimes. And she would tell me not to touch her so much. She knows that she is pretty, but hands off! We always tell our friends and visitors to the house that, if she rolls on her back with her paws together like a kangaroo as if she wants a tummy rub, do not be fooled. It is a trap, for sure!

Maybelline would tell me she does love me, but that daddy is her favorite. Sorry! She would also ask me why she is not allowed in my home office, closets, or other areas around the house. She knows why, though. This is between her and me. If she could talk to Scotty, she would thank him for befriending her, playing with her, and protecting her from Jack and Leeloo.

Daisy is still a kitten and has not said her first meows yet. She purrs and makes a noise as if she is trying to meow. If she could talk, she may tell me where she came from and that she appreciated me taking a chance on her. When Daisy looks at me, I know she is grateful for the home she has, no talking necessary.

CHAPTER 5

The Neighborhood Ferals and the Lost Ones

The term "feral" typically describes something wild. However, many of the feral cats that have come and gone from my house were not wild at all. Although some of them do not allow me to touch or play with them, the bonds I have with these outdoor cats are unique.

We have around seven feral cats that grace us with their presence daily. In the morning, when I wake up and care for my indoor kitties, I then go outside and feed those cats that show up. Usually, I have about five of them come around in the morning: Fu Manchu, Big Head, Skinny Girl, Pretty Eyes, Beautiful, and sometimes, Mr. Kitty. I understand that their names may seem peculiar, but they were given based on their appearances and interactions with me.

My morning schedule includes getting up at around 5:30 a.m. and feeding all six of my inside kitties, cleaning litter pans, and feeding the outside kitties. I find some time in between to make myself some coffee. They all know when it is feeding time. Most of the time, at least two of the outside kitties may show up out front, which are Fu Manchu and Skinny Girl. The others are usually out back. Those are Big Head, Pretty Eyes, Beautiful, and my neighbor's outdoor cat, Mr. Kitty.

Like clockwork, they always stare me down in the window for breakfast, treats, or dinner. Of course, I am a sucker. I give in to them and give them anything they want. I think about how funny I must look when I am outside feeding them, twice or more a day. I spend a great deal of money on disposable bowls, cat food, and treats. But it is from my heart that I provide them with anything they want. I try to anticipate their needs as best I can. I never give my responsibility to them a second thought. They are relying on me to survive.

The most beautiful thing about these cats is that they are all spayed and neutered, and they will always have a home here. The same organization that helped me catch Scotty and his brothers and mother also helped me catch all of these feral cats, took them to the spay and neuter clinic, and got them the care they needed. They were then released back into my yard. This is a crucial step because, if they had been released out into the wild somewhere, they may not have survived. I wish I could rescue all the feral cats that come around, but I know I cannot save all of them. Caring for cats takes a lot of work, and sometimes, it can be overwhelming.

My husband and I have been working on ways to take care of cats for years. We brainstorm ideas to feed them, keep them warm, provide shelter during storms, and protect them from harm, other animals, and diseases. In recent years, we have constructed feeding stations and houses to provide better care for them, while at the same time making it look nice in our yard with shrubs and flowers. But it has certainly been a struggle to try and get it right. The feral cats have helped us understand where they like to eat and where and how they want to sleep. This understanding has helped us put together what works great now.

We have two feeding stations that are covered and are off the ground. They are both outdoor-type wooden dog houses that my husband cut extra doors in so the cats can go in and eat but not feel trapped. They can quickly escape through another opening if something outside attempts to harm them.

Socializing and interacting with feral cats requires patience. However, attempts to this may not always be successful due to their feral nature. Here are some tips for socializing and interacting with feral cats that I have learned along the way from veterinarians, animal advocate organizations, and my personal experience over the years.

Checking on them daily helps build trust. I believe that cats feel more secure when they can anticipate and predict their environment. I try to feed our outside cats at the same times every morning and evening. Of course, feeding times can change based on the season. If it is cold outside, they like to eat earlier, more often, and in bigger portions to help them survive. If I am a few minutes late for mealtime, they are there waiting for me. They expect and trust that I will provide them with food and water. Additionally, with the outside houses we put out each year to keep them warm and dry, we try to make sure that they are placed in areas that are easily accessible, nearby where they had been placed the previous year, and safe from other animals.

I have learned that short, frequent visits work best when interacting with the feral cats in the yard. Sometimes, I will sit nearby and watch them eat while knowing if they seem to trust me or are scared. I pay close attention to each cat's body language and try to avoid making contact with it. I have learned that speaking softly and slowly to a cat helps it get accustomed to your voice. And, of course, food helps build a trusting relationship.

I have been lucky to care for so many wonderful felines. I want to share the stories and beautiful pictures of the feral cats that currently roam around my house, and those who are no longer with us but have left a lasting impact on my heart. I hope you enjoy reading their stories and embracing their beauty.

Fu Manchu

Fu Manchu got his name because of his drooping whiskers, which remind me of an older Chinese man. He is a gray tabby cat who has been visiting our house for almost seven years. He positions himself near the front door every morning and starts meowing as I exit with his food. Although he is older, he is very vocal. Sometimes, his meow sounds like a baby crying, which sometimes gets louder.

Fu, as I call him for short, usually hangs out with Skinny Girl, Pretty Eyes, and sometimes Big Head. He takes his time walking around, and I can tell he is getting old and must have a few aches and pains. He is neutered, has his rabies shot, and is well-fed with vitamins and great daily food from my house. I love spending time with him in the backyard, where I will sit and talk to him—asking him if he is OK. He trusts me and has never been scared away because he knows I mean no harm.

In the past, Fu only visited my yard for short periods. However, lately, he has been staying around daily. We provide him with a cozy heated bed in the winter, and he can lounge wherever he pleases in the spring and summer. Even when I bring my two dogs, Suki and Sally, outside, Fu tolerates them. He watches them run around, relaxes, and closes his eyes as if he is very comfortable and knows that we mean him no harm. This makes me feel great. Luckily, my dogs love cats and do not bother Fu. Knowing that Fu is comfortable around my house and feels safe is a relief because, as long as he stays here, he will live very long.

Mr. Tan

Around 2012, a feral cat we later named Mr. Tan, or Tough as Nails, entered our yard. He had a round face and noticeably short ears, which we eventually learned were characteristic of the Scottish Fold breed. Unfortunately, he had a deep scar around his neck that went all the way around. He also had scratches on his face, and his skin was coming off, making it hard for him to walk. It was evident that something or someone had hurt him. I could not be sure, but the look of the wound seemed intentional. I always thought that a human had hurt him, but I could not be sure. It was heart-wrenching to see him in such a condition, and every time we saw him, we would tear up. If we had known more about his condition and how to get him trapped and taken in to see someone, we would have helped him earlier.

Despite his condition, Mr. Tan continued to come and go as he pleased, and we fed him two to three times a day. Eventually, he started to heal, but we still could not touch or hold him. He had most likely fathered many kittens in his life, but we could not capture him to take him in for neutering until later. We also got him a rabies shot and antibiotics. Looking back, it hurts to think about how he was back then, but he was old. I always wanted to do more. I just wanted to pick him up and tell him it was OK, but I could not.

Before he passed away, Mr. Tan looked worse than he ever had. He looked sick, his eyes were watering, and he would not eat. One day, he left our yard and never came back. We knew that he had gone off to pass away quietly, but I went around the neighborhood and some of the other streets near us to look for him, but I could not find him. I am tearing up just writing this, but he was as tough as nails up until the end, and I am happy that I could provide shelter, food, and a safe environment for him to roam. I think about him every day, and I look out my front door at the other kitties that come and go. Sometimes, I think he will show up, but I know he will not. It was even harder throwing the blankets away that were in the outside cat house where he would sleep. I could still smell him, even though I could never touch him.

Mr. Tan, I miss you.

Mama Kitty

Mama Kitty was one of the first feral cats we ever took care of outside. She was a beautiful cat with soft, gentle eyes and a soft, gray coat. Her eyes thanked us for everything we did for her whenever she looked at us. She would come to our yard every day to eat and relax. However, Mama Kitty was not spayed, so she had many kittens over the years. She would bring her kittens around to show them where to eat; before we knew it, they would be on their own. Some would stay around; some would leave, and we would not see them for months. I believe many of the other cats around now could be her offspring.

Mama Kitty used to wander around the neighborhood to nap and have her kittens running around. My neighbor would send me pictures of the kittens playing on her porch while Mama Kitty rested. I believe that, because other cats frequented our yard, Mama Kitty wanted to make sure her kittens were safe and decided to take them somewhere else.

A few years ago, Mama Kitty passed away. Unfortunately, she was pregnant and had miscarried. We took her to the animal urgent care, but they could not save her, so we had her cremated and put her remains in a special box with her name on it.

Big Head

The name Big Head might sound unkind, but you would understand if you saw this cat. His head is incredibly big and round. I sometimes wonder if he and Fu are related, but I cannot be sure, as so many cats have come around over the years. He is generally a solitary cat and does not trust me enough to come too close. He keeps his distance when I feed him but stays in our yard, for the most part. We always ensure that he has a warm and cozy place to sleep in one of our outdoor cat houses during the winter. Big Head is a lot smarter than most of the cats that come around. He sleeps there every night, and if it is raining, he takes shelter there too. We have also had him neutered and given a rabies shot.

Big Head often spends time with Beautiful, one of the female cats that visit daily. She is a small, dark-gray and mostly white cat who is also spayed and has received a rabies shot. Big Head is a mystery because he does not stay around too much while I feed him, so I am unable to get to know him like I want to. If I sit down near him, he is more nervous than most of the other cats. However, he knows I care about him a lot.

Pretty Girl

Pretty Girl earned her name due to her soft, stunning face, beautiful eyes, and light-gray coat. Her graceful movements, melodious meows, and friendly interactions with other out-side cats also contribute to why I affectionately call her Pretty Girl. She usually spends her time with Big Head, but sometimes, she is seen with Fu and Skinny Girl.

Every morning, when I open the garage to feed them, Pretty Girl runs toward me from the driveway. Although I am unsure where she sleeps, or if she has a home to go to, she appears to be in good health despite being a little plump around the edges. Usually, when I feed the cats outside, my dogs join me. Pretty Girl always starts to walk close to Suki, my biggest but youngest dog, as if she is trying to bond or say hello. Sometimes, she even meows as she gets closer.

Pretty Girl is also a hunter. On many occasions, I have looked out the door and seen her staring at the grass, and then suddenly, she takes one of her paws and pushes it into a place in the yard. She is searching for moles.

Skinny Girl

Whenever I think about Skinny Girl, it brings a smile to my face. Even though the name Skinny Girl might not be the best choice for a female cat, we gave her this name because she was skinny when she first visited us. The name just stuck with her as she continued to come around daily. Of course, she has gained a lot more weight over the past few years, and the name may not suit her that well, but she listens when I say it, so I will keep calling her that.

Skinny Girl has large eyes that appear crossed when she looks at you. She seems very fond of Fu, as they always walk around together and share meals. They are quite affectionate with each other and are often seen rubbing against each other or even sleeping in the same outside cat house. When I am in the garage with the main or side door open, she peeks in to watch me prepare their food. She always comes into the garage and lays down until I give her the food. I love it that she is OK with my presence. When I feed her in front of our house, she darts toward the door while I am coming out and takes a sneak peek inside as if seeing if there is room for her in the Vaden house.

Grayson

Grayson is a male cat with short, gray hair. He first appeared in our yard in June 2023. This year was significant because Grayson had been away from his natural home for an unusually long time, since 2021. At first, I thought he was just another feral cat looking for food. But then, he started to get close to me. He would rub against my leg, meow, and even try to follow me inside my house.

I knew this cat was different and may have roamed from his home. I could tell he was neutered, but to make sure, I sent a picture of him to my veterinarian for confirmation. Dr. Jenny Powers, who deserves her chapter in this book for all she has done for us and our animals, confirmed his neutering and suggested checking for a microchip to identify his owner. Since I thought capturing him and taking him to the vet would be difficult, my husband ordered a chip reader online.

One afternoon, I waited for Grayson to enter the garage. He eventually walked up to me and hopped on my lap. I used the chip reader to scan his back, from his neck to his tail, and it beeped! He had a chip with a unique number. I immediately wrote down the number and used the microchip registry website (https://www.aaha.org/) to find out which company was associated with it. I contacted the company with the number, and they confirmed that the cat's owner was in South Carolina. I was in North Carolina, so I initially wondered about the validity of the information. However, they said they would call the owner on file and have them contact me if the information was valid.

That day, the owners called me from South Carolina and confirmed that the cat they called Grayson belonged to them but had been missing since 2021. It was now 2023! I was shocked and could not believe it. I asked if they wanted me to send pictures to verify his identity, and they agreed. They also said they would drive to my location to pick up Grayson in a few hours. I was overwhelmed with emotions and cried tears of joy at the miracle that had just occurred.

Grayson was healthy and handsome, as if he had never left home. I wanted to keep him safe and settled in the garage until his owners arrived. When they finally arrived, Grayson went right to them, and they were overjoyed to have him back. I was nervous that something might go wrong, but fortunately, everything went smoothly, and I was happy that I could help reunite them.

Currently, Grayson is happy and safe with his family, and my husband and I have made new friends through this experience. His story is nothing short of a beautiful miracle; I always keep him in my thoughts. His parents send me pictures and updates on how he is doing, and I am grateful to have a connection with him. You will hear more about him later.

Sonny

The story of Sonny is an even more special one. When Sonny wandered into our yard, he was quite friendly but did not have a microchip or collar. He was affectionate and would stay around to eat and sleep. I considered bringing him into our home, but since all of our cats were older, it would not have been fair to them or him. So I had to produce a plan to ensure that he would find a loving home. Fortunately, there are many cat lovers in my area, so it was easy for me to spread the word. After months of searching for a home for him, I was finally able to find one with a woman named Carole. In the process, I gained a lifelong friend.

The Black-and-White Cat

A cat known only as The Black-and-White Cat has been visiting our house for several years. We usually see him at night when he comes around for a bite. Sometimes, I would look out the front window and see him trotting across the cul-de-sac toward our house. Unfortunately, I could never get a good picture of him. I smile because I have always believed he has a home somewhere. After all, he is pretty chunky. But I love that he knows where to come for food and shelter.

The Fluffy Orange Cat

One day, I was looking out my front door and saw a fluffy orange cat trotting across the road toward my house. It had long, flowing fur and short legs. It seemed like it was on a mission, but it stopped every few feet to take in the smells on the pavement. As it got closer, I wondered why it was coming over. I thought it must be because of the food, so I opened the door to see if there was any food out front, in case it was hungry. Suddenly, it stopped in its tracks, looked at me, and ran underneath one of our cars parked out front. I went back inside and peeked out the window to see if it would continue its journey toward the front door. And it did. It ran up the steps quickly, looking around to ensure nothing was coming up on it, and started eating the food as fast as possible.

The fluffy orange cat looked healthy, and I thought it belonged to someone and was coming for extra food. After finishing its food, it slowly walked down the front steps and stopped for a minute to wash its paws and lick a few areas of fur before trotting away in the same direction it had come from. This fluffy orange cat comes around occasionally, usually in the middle of the day. Although, I have not seen it lately. I hope that someone is taking care of it.

Beautiful

Beautiful is a female white, gray, and black tabby who was part of the original cats that we trapped. She visits our home mostly in the morning looking for breakfast with her pal Big Head. Once in a while she will venture out and come around at night. When I am about to feed her, she meows at me a few times as if she is grateful. I love seeing her in the morning because she is so beautiful.

CHAPTER
6

Important Information for Cat Owners

A Long-Term Commitment

There is no denying that owning a cat comes with significant responsibility, whether you have a domesticated cat or a rescue. Unfortunately, many cats endure neglect, abuse, abandonment, and homelessness. Stray and feral cats often struggle to survive in tough conditions, facing hunger, disease, and the dangers of traffic and predators. Rescuing cats involves giving them a chance at a better life, free from suffering and fear. It is a noble and rewarding endeavor that can significantly impact the lives of these beloved animals.

Understanding the significance of cat rescue and the rescue process is essential. By acknowledging the challenges and rewards of cat rescue, individuals can make a positive difference in these vulnerable animals' lives and contribute to creating a more compassionate society. Furthermore, cat rescue helps communities by managing feral cat populations through trap-neuter-return (TNR) programs.

Trapping feral cats and getting them the assistance and checkups they need can be a challenging task. Some individuals may feel uneasy about trapping cats, fearing they may get hurt or run away. However, with the help of local cat coalitions, individuals can participate in TNR programs and learn how to safely trap and release cats back into their environments. Supporting TNR programs is an excellent way to manage feral cat populations and improve their quality of life.

Decoding Cat Behavior

I have spent a significant amount of time learning about cat behavior. I have read several books and articles and have sought advice from professionals and cat organizations. However, there is still a lot more to comprehend and learn. I have not decoded it yet! However, I have come to understand that cats are generally independent animals that prefer to spend their time in quiet and secluded areas. This can make it difficult to comprehend their motives and behaviors. My cats, for instance, enjoy having their own hiding places, such as under the bed, in a closet, or even in a cat tower that provides privacy. They are sometimes great at hiding, and I admit I have spent time looking for them while they were hiding close by.

Cats are natural hunters, and many of their behaviors are rooted in their predatory instincts. Cats are also territorial animals and can exhibit complex behaviors such as marking and defending their territory. I have experienced this firsthand, given that I have three cats at home who have taken it upon themselves to mark or spray in an area. However, it is best to address this behavior early on, or you might end up with a real problem on your hands—or walls. Fortunately, I have been pretty good at deterring this behavior.

While some aspects of cat behavior may resemble pack mentality, cats' social structures and behaviors differ from those of pack animals like wolves. Each cat's personality and individual experiences significantly shape their behavior within a group.

Developing a relationship with cats requires earning their trust and bonding with them emotionally and physically. It entails understanding their preferences, likes, dislikes, and overall behavior. For instance, a meow can be a greeting, while a deep growl could signify anger or discomfort. Understanding a cat's traits and preferences can help in interpreting its behavior. Owners can learn more about their feline companions by paying attention to signals such as the position and movement of a cat's tail and even its ears.

Each cat has a unique personality and temperament. While some may argue that cats are selfish and loners, they are affectionate and giving creatures. They demonstrate their love toward their owners in various ways, such as purring, kneading, headbutting, and rubbing against them.

Developing close relationships with cats involves physical affection, closeness, and shared routines, such as feeding times, playtime, and relaxation. Cats are often cherished as companions because of their independent yet affectionate nature. They provide comfort, emotional support, and a sense of companionship to their owners.

Mischievous Kitties

Cats are more active at night, which can lead to behaviors that seem puzzling. Cats are known for their curious and mischievous behavior, and some cats habitually "steal" items around the house. This behavior often involves cats picking up and carrying off small objects such as socks, toys, or other items, and it can occur at any time, including at night.

Cats sometimes indulge in nighttime activities because they are being playful. While it may seem like the cat is "stealing," they usually follow their instincts and exhibit playful or hunting behaviors. Cats are natural hunters, and picking up and carrying objects can mimic the behavior of catching prey. They may also be looking to get attention. If they notice that their behavior gets a reaction, such as being chased or receiving attention, they may continue to do it for the response.

Some cats may carry around soft items like socks or small plush toys to create a sense of comfort or security. These items may remind them of their mother or help them feel more secure in their environment. Make sure your cat has plenty of appropriate toys to play with. Interactive toys, puzzle feeders, and toys that mimic prey can help satisfy your cat's hunting instincts. Keep small, valuable, or potentially dangerous items out of your cat's reach. This can help prevent them from carrying off items that could be harmful if ingested. Also, if you have dogs that like to chew the insides out of all the toys you buy (as I do), please ensure the little cat toys are also put away.

Strategies for a Peaceful Multicat Home

If you have multiple cats living together, ensuring their living environment is stress-free and enjoyable for all is important. While cats can coexist peacefully, it requires patience, training, and understanding from their human companions. Here are some helpful tips to promote harmony among your feline friends.

Living with multiple cats has been a unique and rewarding experience for me. It is full of many responsibilities and challenges, and of course, I am never lonely and am always entertained. Just like children, they make messes and cry for attention, and I am always there to help them.

If you have multiple cats, ensure they have enough space to move around comfortably. My husband and I are fortunate to have a large home, and the cats have freedom to roam. They also have quiet spaces around the house where they can go individually to take their much-needed naps.

It is costly to house, feed, and provide health care for multiple cats. My husband and I always joke that we spend our retirement savings on the cats and dogs we have. But we would sell our souls to keep them happy and healthy. There is nothing that we would not do for them. But taking care of multiple cats is not just about money; it is also about dedication and patience.

Dealing with the Dreaded Litter Box

Phew! All of us cat ladies know that the litter box can be a dreaded thing to empty every day, especially if you have a multicat household. However, one crucial aspect of feline care is providing a clean and suitable litter box for the cats to use—unless you have been able to train your smart little felines to use the human potty. But seriously, the litter box is vital in maintaining a healthy environment for the cats and their human family members.

As a cat lady with multiple cats, I put great importance on the cleanliness of the litter boxes. The truth is, cats are naturally clean animals with a strong instinct to bury their poop and pee, and if they have a litter box that fulfills this instinctual behavior and helps to prevent accidents around the house, they will be very happy. And I will, too!

Cats are also sensitive to smells, and a dirty litter box can lead to aversion and refusal to use it. I have a few cats that will first smell the litter box before they enter. I also have a few that will wait outside the door until I finish cleaning it out. The type of litter used in the litter box also plays a significant role in the cat's comfort and acceptance of the box. There are various types of cat litter available on the market, including clumping, nonclumping, and natural alternatives like wood pellets. Each cat may have a preference for a specific type of litter, so it may require some experimentation to find the most suitable option for each of your feline companions. In addition to maintaining cleanliness and hygiene, the placement of the litter box is crucial for the cat's comfort and convenience.

Cats prefer privacy and quiet when using the litter box, so it is best to place it in a quiet and easily accessible location. Avoid placing the litter box near the cat's food and water bowls, as cats prefer to keep their elimination area separate from their feeding area. I have my downstairs litter boxes in our laundry room, which is quiet and private. The upstairs two are in a guest bathroom, which is also quiet and private.

Furthermore, the number of litter boxes in a household should correspond to the number of cats. The general rule is to have one litter box per cat, plus an additional box to prevent competition and territorial issues.

Providing multiple litter boxes in different areas of the house gives cats options and ensures that they always have a clean and available space to use when needed. In conclusion, the cat litter box is an essential component of feline care that contributes to the health and well-being of our feline companions.

By understanding the importance of a clean litter box, choosing the right type of litter, and maintaining proper hygiene and placement, cat owners can create a comfortable and inviting environment for their cats. A well-maintained litter box benefits the cat and enhances the harmony and happiness of the entire household.

The Feline Necessities

Like the dreaded litter box, the feline food bowl is also important, but much less messy. Whether you have one cat or multiple, providing the best food and nutrition is very important. Of course, if you have multiple cats (like I do), you also have multiple food bowls. I have been lucky that my inside cats eat together pretty well. I feed them in the morning, and they usually eat what is left throughout the day. Additionally, feeding your cats separately using individual food and water bowls is recommended to prevent conflicts.

Give your cats something to climb or perch on, such as cat towers, and set up multiple hiding spots to make them feel safe and secure. Regularly playing with your cats keeps them active and mentally stimulated. Encourage positive socialization among your cats, but be prepared to intervene and separate them if conflicts arise. Additionally, providing scratching posts will prevent your cats from scratching your furniture and will give them a place to mark their territory. Monitor your cats' behaviors to identify signs of tension or aggression, and address any issues early to prevent escalation.

Microchips and Collars

Proper identification is important in case a cat gets lost, as you have just read in the story about Grayson. The love and companionship that cats bring to our lives are invaluable. At our home, we ensure that all our cats wear collars with their names and have microchips implanted, just in case they wander off and get lost. Additionally, we put bells on their collars to help us locate them if they are hiding in the house. This is very important in case of a fire or in an emergency situation.

A microchip is a small electronic device implanted under a cat's skin, usually between the shoulder blades. This chip contains a unique identification number that can be scanned by a vet or an animal shelter if the cat becomes lost. You can also purchase microchips online. They have been invaluable tools for my husband and me, with the many feral cats that come through. By having a microchip implanted, the chance of reuniting a lost cat with its owner significantly increases.

Another important tool is a collar with an identification tag that includes the cat's name and the owner's contact information. If someone finds a lost cat, they can easily contact the owner by reading the information on the tag. Providing a cat with both a microchip and a collar with an ID tag ensures that they have a double layer of protection.

Veterinarian Visits

Did you know that cats are experts at hiding signs of illness? That is why taking your furry feline for regular vet checkups is important. These exams can help catch any health issues early on, before they become harder to treat. Having six cats and the responsibility of scheduling yearly exams, and sometimes having unexpected visits to the vet, can be overwhelming and even costly. However, having yearly exams is important for preventive care.

Cats can become anxious or fearful when taken to the vet because of the unfamiliar environment, sounds, and even scents. Some cats may try to hide or become defensive, while others may become aggressive toward the veterinarian or their staff due to fear or stress.

Cats may also meow or vocalize loudly when they are upset. Additionally, they may urinate out of fear or stress during the visit.

My husband and I have been fortunate to have what we call the best veterinarian around. Dr. Jenny Powers has cared for our fur babies for twelve or more years. She has watched them grow up and has done everything possible to make sure they live long and healthy lives. Although we have had other veterinarians who have helped us tremendously, she is one that we count on, and our animals count on. We will forever be grateful for the love, care, and attention she has given to our animals. The relationship you and your felines, or other animals, have with the veterinarian is as important as the one you have with your own doctor.

Grooming and Dental Care

Keeping your cat well-groomed is essential to maintaining its coat and skin health, and promoting comfort and relaxation. My cats love regular brushing to remove excess hair. Some of them even enjoy a waterless bath using fragrant grooming shampoos. Brushing them helps remove hair where they are shedding, which can reduce hair balls and other digestive problems that may occur. Also, keeping their eyes clean and their nails trimmed is very important.

If you have never brought your cat in for a dental exam and cleaning, you should. When Te came into our lives, because of the FIV, his body, of course, could not absorb all the many things he needed to have strong teeth or even a healthy coat. So we took him in for dental exams and a cleaning each year. Although he lost a few teeth because of the disease, they were clean and promoted a healthier lifestyle for him.

Playtime

Entertaining cats can be challenging, but keeping them physically and mentally engaged is essential. I provide my cats with toys, scratching posts, and lots of catnip, which helps them relax. Watching them play with their favorite toys is always fun and keeps them engaged and active. During Christmas, my husband and I enjoy seeing our cats play with toys, especially small cat toys with catnip on them. We even take pictures of them and have fun!

Traveling with Feline Companions

I have had a lot of experience traveling with most of my cats. I was commuting to a job during the week and would take some of my cats with me because I missed them, and my husband had to work full time. Looking back, I did not put them in a carrier or anything, which I should have done for their safety. However, I would put a cat tower, blankets, and a small litter box in the back for them to use if needed. And they would use it. I remember the first time I heard one of them scratching in the litter. I was so happy. They just seemed to know that was what they needed to do.

During the two years I commuted, it was always a smooth journey. My cat Te would sit in my lap, and Jack would sit on the middle console in the front and look out the window.

Leeloo would stay on the cat tower, and Lana would sleep on the floor in the back seat. When I arrived at the house I was renting, I would pull into the garage and close the door. I would then open the van door, and they would all head toward the back door. They were so very smart.

Traveling with cats can be challenging, whether it's a short trip to the veterinarian or a long journey to a new home. Cats are known for their independent nature and sensitivity to environmental changes, making them prone to stress and anxiety during travel.

When traveling with cats in a car or another mode of transportation, it is essential to prioritize their safety and well-being. I should have definitely been more safety-minded when it came to them being in the car in a carrier. Based on my experience during those few years, here are some of my tips for traveling with cats.

One of the most important things you can do to ensure your cat's safety during travel is to use a secure and well-ventilated carrier so that it will not move back and forth. I would always make sure my music was calming, and I made sure to drive safely.

To help keep your cat calm during the journey, create a comfortable travel environment inside the carrier. Line the bottom with a soft blanket or towel, and include familiar items such as your cat's favorite toys or clothing with your scent to provide a sense of security.

To prevent motion sickness and discomfort, avoid feeding your cat a large meal before traveling. Offer a light meal a few hours before the journey, to reduce the risk of nausea and vomiting.

Keep an eye on your cat throughout the trip to ensure it is comfortable and not showing signs of distress. If your cat seems anxious or agitated, try to reassure it by speaking to it calmly and soothingly. Suppose your cat becomes nervous or agitated while traveling in a carrier. In that case, you may consult your veterinarian about potential solutions to help alleviate stress, such as pheromone sprays or calming supplements.

In conclusion, traveling with cats requires careful planning and consideration to ensure their safety and well-being. By following these tips and taking the necessary precautions, you can help make the travel experience more comfortable and stress-free for your feline companion.

The Bad and the Ugly of Declawing a Cat

Declawing a cat, also known as onychectomy, is a surgical procedure involving amputating a cat's claws and the last bone of each toe. While some may consider declawing as a solution to prevent furniture damage or scratches, it is essential to be aware of this procedure's potential negative consequences.

Declawing involves removing a vital part of a cat's anatomy, purely for human convenience. Many animal welfare organizations and veterinarians advocate against declawing, a nonessential and potentially harmful procedure. I have never thought about declawing my cats.

The Bad

Pain and Discomfort: Declawing is a painful procedure for cats, as it involves cutting through bones, nerves, and tendons. Cats may experience pain during and after the surgery, leading to complications such as infection, swelling, and prolonged discomfort. Getting a regular trim is the best thing to do.

Behavioral Changes: Declawing can significantly impact a cat's behavior. Cats rely on their claws for scratching, stretching, and climbing. Removing their claws can lead to behavioral issues like aggression, litter box avoidance, and increased anxiety.

Defenselessness: Claws are essential for a cat's defense mechanism in the wild and in domestic settings. Declawed cats cannot protect themselves effectively if they encounter threats or predators, increasing vulnerability and stress.

The Ugly

Long-Term Health Risks: Declawing cats can lead to long-term health problems. The procedure can cause changes in their anatomy that result in chronic pain, arthritis, and altered walking patterns. These health issues can significantly impact the cat's quality of life.

Psychological Effects: Declawing cats can negatively impact their emotional well-being by depriving them of their natural behaviors and coping mechanisms. This can lead to symptoms of depression, fear, and stress, ultimately affecting their overall mental health.

While declawing may seem like a quick fix for cat owners dealing with scratching issues, it is essential to consider this procedure's negative consequences and ethical implications. Alternative methods—such as providing scratching posts, trimming nails, and following behavior modification techniques—can help address scratching behavior without resorting to declawing. Prioritizing their well-being and natural behaviors is crucial in fostering a healthy and harmonious relationships between cats and their human companions.

Dealing with the Loss of a Pet

Losing a pet can be the hardest thing to deal with. Take it from me. Everyone deals with death differently, and some not at all. But, if you are seeking ways to help you deal with the loss of a pet, below are some suggestions to get you there. These are some of the ways that I have dealt with losing my dog, Boot, and my cats, Te and Mr. Tan, as well as Mama Kitty.

First, you have to allow yourself to grieve your furry friend. Feeling sad, angry, guilty, or even numb is normal. Accepting your emotions can help you work through them.

Reach out for support from your friends and family members who understand the bond you shared with your pet. It is very comforting to me when I share my feelings with others, especially if they have pets as well.

I already shared that, when Boot passed away, it was the hardest loss for me. However, my husband helped create a memorial of sorts for Boot. He was cremated, and we got a beautiful box and an angel figurine and put his collar in the box. It was wonderful. We also framed one of the best pictures of Boot, when he was happier and healthier. Today, it is in our library, right next to Te, who was his only companion at the time.

For some, losing a pet is like losing a child or another family member. It can take an emotional and physical toll on us. So it is important to make sure that you take care of yourself and relax. However, if you are struggling and are having a terrible time coping, maybe consider reaching out to a professional or a friend to talk through your grief.

Finally, it has helped me when I focus on the happy times and interactions with my pet, rather than on the tragedy that has happened. Give yourself time. Healing from the loss of a pet takes time, and everyone processes grief differently.

CHAPTER
7

Heartwarming Stories from the Cat Lady Network

Cats have an incredible ability to touch our hearts in unexpected ways. Their playful behavior and unwavering companionship have inspired countless stories of love and resilience. In this chapter, I am excited to share heartwarming stories from some of my closest feline-loving friends and neighbors. The stories cover various cat-related topics, such as reuniting lost cats with their families, welcoming cats into one's life, and the special bonds between humans and cats. They also showcase the profound depth and significance of their relationships with these creatures, highlighting the joy, comfort, and love they bring into our lives. I hope they leave you with a warm heart and a renewed appreciation for the love of cats.

Carmen's Beloved Cats

Callie, Tassie, Felix, and Grayson

Carmen loves cats a lot. Although she likes dogs, cats make her feel calm, and her kids adore them also. It makes her so happy to see her love of cats mirrored in her two boys. They even call her a cat whisperer because all their kitties will come to her when she calls them. She knows precisely what each cat likes and does not like, so they know exactly what they are getting from her. Carmen communicates with her kitties with her unique sounds, such as *pssspp*, clicking, and kisses. She even headbutts a lot with them.

Cats were always part of Carmen's life. Her granddad had an orange tabby that would guard her crib and alert anyone to her crying or making noise. His name was TT. When she was five, one of her neighbors found a kitten in a dumpster. It was a calico cat they named Scruffy because Carmen's mom thought it was scruffy-looking from being in the dumpster. Once Scruffy got all of her veterinarian visits and necessary medications, she transformed into a beautiful cat with a gorgeous coat.

Unfortunately, at the age of ten, Scruffy had tumors surrounding her heart, so Carmen and her family had to let her go. They were heartbroken. Once Carmen went to college, she wanted a cat so badly. She lived by herself in an apartment and thought a cat would be great company for her, and she missed Scruffy so much. However, she could not commit to adopting a cat that may have high veterinarian bills because she was working part time. Surprisingly, on Christmas in 1999, her family gave her a wonderful present. They gave her a box of cat toys and told her to go ahead and find a cat that she wanted to adopt, and they would help her with the veterinarian bills and other costs until she graduated and had a full-time job.

Carmen started searching and found Callie in a newspaper ad that following February. When she picked her up, she was five weeks old; she curled up in her hand and started purring. Callie was a tortoiseshell cat. Although Callie was most likely too young to be separated from her mom and her littermates at the time, the family had to give them all away, so Carmen took care of her.

Felix and Grayson.

Over the years, Callie was a constant source of support and comfort for Carmen through many significant events in her life, but unfortunately, she passed away suddenly in October 2016. This loss devastated Carmen and her family, and they found it difficult to consider getting another cat for over a year.

In March 2018, Carmen found a photo of Tassie on the local humane society's website. The cat reminded her so much of their previous cat, Callie, that she called her husband to bring their two young sons to meet Tassie. However, Carmen was worried because tortoiseshell cats are known for not being very accepting. To her delight, Tassie liked the kids and even allowed them to pick her up. She purred contentedly. They filled out the adoption papers that same night and brought her home. Tassie loves to snuggle. She sleeps either on top of Carmen or on her pillow; she also likes to sit on Carmen's or her husband's chest while they watch TV, and she supervises the kids while they're getting ready for school each morning. Tassie also likes to solar charge on the screened porch.

Felix.

In November 2018, Carmen and her two boys went to PetSmart to buy cat food for their cat, Tassie. While they were there, they came across an adoption event and brought home a gray kitten named Starry, who would later be renamed Grayson. Grayson had been found on one of the interstates and brought to the adoption service. Although he was very skittish, he got along well with Tassie. However, he did not like being around Carmen's young boys because they were loud, so he tended to hang out with Carmen and her husband when the kids went to bed. Despite this, Grayson was the sweetest boy. He made biscuits beside Carmen and liked to rub all over her. He would get his head under her arm and force her to pet him. He had the loudest purrs, and when he was really happy and relaxed, he drooled a lot.

Grayson.

In February 2021, Grayson went missing. The door from their garage into the house had been left open, and the garage door had happened to be open, too, so they thought he had taken off. Carmen and her family made flyers, posted notifications on social media sites, and searched neighborhoods, but unfortunately, they never found him. Carmen and her family were heartbroken.

A month later, Carmen spotted Felix, a snowshoe cat, on the local humane society's website. She was shocked that a snowshoe cat was there; they are a rare breed. The COVID-19 pandemic was taking place at the time, so when she drove to the humane society, she had to wait in the car to meet him. She waited two hours to go in and see Felix, and he crawled into her lap and started playing. She brought him home that night. She surprised her kids, who were very happy when Felix was so playful and responsive. He loves to chase feathers, lasers, and treat toys. He is definitely a hunter and a wannabe outdoor kitty. His favorite spot is on the screened porch in his cat tree, which looks like a tree! Felix and Tassie are not close friends. While Felix wants to play and wrestle, Tassie does not share the same enthusiasm.

Tassie and Grayson.

On Father's Day in 2023, Carmen received an unexpected phone call. It was revealed that Grayson's microchip had been activated, and he had been located in Pinehurst, North Carolina. Grayson had started visiting a family that looked after some feral cats and the family had realized that he was not feral. They were able to scan his microchip, and luckily, Carmen's contact number popped up in the results. Carmen started crying when she saw that Grayson had been found. She and her husband drove from Greenville, South Carolina, to Pinehurst to pick him up that same day.

Carmen and her family thought hard about how Grayson could have ended up in Pinehurst, North Carolina. They figured that he had likely gotten stuck under the hood of their car, because the weekend after he had gone missing, she and her husband had taken a trip with friends to Pinehurst. That was the only explanation they could devise for how he had gotten there.

When Carmen got Grayson home, she took him to the veterinarian, updated his shots, and reintroduced him to Tassie, his sister, and his new brother, Felix. Tassie was not impressed, but Felix was super excited to have a play friend. They love to wrestle and chase each other all over the house.

When Grayson disappeared, Carmen could not bring herself to get rid of any of his belongings. As a result, she still had his old bed that he also sleeps in now. Before he went missing, she'd had Christmas stockings made for the family, and she is happy to be able to use Grayson's stocking again. Carmen has noticed that Grayson is not as nervous as he used to be. He enjoys spending time with her children, sleeps with them sometimes, and later comes to her room at night. Since his return, Grayson has shown no interest in going outside. Perhaps he is not as excited about the outdoors as he used to be, having lived outside for a while. He is the same sweet and affectionate cat that Carmen and her family remember.

Kelly Clyde: Anne's Comfort Cat

Kelly Clyde

Kelly Clyde is a handsome tuxedo cat with unique black-and-white markings and a charming personality. Anne affectionately refers to him as her "gentleman" cat. He is approximately four years old and is Anne's first indoor cat. She named him after her son's cat, Kelly, whom she had taken care of for a while and become attached to but had to return.

Kelly Clyde.

Kelly Clyde was originally named Carlos by the animal advocacy organization he was adopted from. But Anne knew he would be her Kelly Clyde. He looked a lot like her son's cat, which made it even more special. She chose his middle name, Clyde, because his big paws reminded her of the feet of a Clydesdale horse, adding a unique and distinguished touch to his name.

Anne takes great care of Kelly Clyde by providing him everything he needs to be happy and healthy. He has a beautiful, spacious home to roam around, with large windows that allow him to watch the birds and squirrels outside, and he has a comfortable bed to rest in. Kelly Clyde enjoys watching animal TV shows, and one of his favorite movies is *Madagascar*. He also loves playing with his numerous cat toys and sitting in his cat tower by the front window.

Anne considers herself lucky to have found Kelly Clyde during a difficult and personal phase in her life. He provided her with the comfort and solace she needed, and in turn, she gave him a forever home. She is excited to strengthen her bond with her beloved feline companion and looks forward to all the adventures they will share together.

Carole's Feline Companions

Limited, Klondike, Squirt, and Sonny

This is a heartwarming story about four cats that have been a source of love, security, warmth, and companionship in Carole's life. Their names are Limited, Klondike, Squirt, and Sonny, each reflecting their unique personalities and how they came to be a part of Carole's life. These feline companions have been a constant source of joy and affection, brightening Carole's life with their presence.

Limited was a female cat named after the company her then-husband worked for, The Limited. Limited was a beautiful gray rescue cat that Carole's husband thought would be a good companion while he was traveling. It was a difficult time for Carole, as she was giving up a job she really enjoyed for their first corporate transfer. Limited definitely provided the comfort she needed during this difficult time.

Limited was an affectionate cat who loved to lay across Carole's shoulders when she sat to read and above her head to sleep. She was definitely *her* cat. Carole indicated that, one day, Limited had accidentally gotten out and had shown up around a week later on her deck. She had the patio door open, and in he came. "But she wasn't alone; a baby rabbit, still alive, was in her mouth." When Carole closed the patio door, Limited dropped the rabbit, which then proceeded to hop around the dining table. Limited and Carole chased after it. Carole went to the kitchen and picked up a box with a lid, and then used the box to successfully capture the bunny. As a result, the bunny survived another day, and Limited was never able to escape again. Sadly, at the age of fourteen, Limited passed away due to urinary issues.

Klondike was a female cat with black and white fur. She was named after the ice cream bar because of her colors. Klondike loved to travel and always accompanied Carole and her family wherever they went. She was a beloved family cat that Carole's children grew up with. Klondike had a sweet and friendly personality and was very affectionate. Sadly, she passed away from urinary issues at the age of fourteen.

Squirt.

Squirt was an orange tabby cat who was very small, hence the name Squirt that was given to him. Carole came across Squirt in her local newspaper's "Pet of the Week" section. When she saw the beautiful, orange tabby, she said she "instantly fell in love and brought him home the same day."

Squirt, despite being a small cat, had a huge personality and a big heart. He was extremely sociable and loved being around people. In fact, he would even greet people at the door, displaying affection and warmth. Carole believes that he might have been a dog in his previous life, as he would approach people in a manner that was uncharacteristic of most cats. Squirt was a loving pet who showed affection to everyone, even dogs.

Most animals are unhappy about visits to the veterinarian, but not Squirt; he loved going to the vet. He even liked to have his nails trimmed. He would not put up a fuss at all. Carole was very lucky to have him in her life. Sometimes, she would use the vacuum to softly remove his excess fur, and he loved it. The noise nor the suction bothered him. He considered it relaxing affection.

Breakfast, lunch, or dinner, Squirt had a place at the table. He would politely sit in his chair as Carole and her husband ate their meals. He wanted to be with them no matter where they were. Like most of Carole's feline friends in her life, Squirt was also a traveler. Probably the best one. He would ride in the car outside his carrier, sometimes laying in the back window, behind Carole's head as she was driving, or beside her, all the while looking out the window. Happy to be wherever Carole was.

Carole considered Squirt a "rare gem," an amazing cat with a special place in her heart. Despite receiving the best veterinarian care, Squirt developed kidney disease and passed away at the age of almost twenty. Carole and her husband were devastated by his loss, which she described as "unimaginable." Losing a feline friend, who is often like a child or companion, can be incredibly difficult to bear.

Carole was already dealing with the loss of her beloved pet, Squirt, when tragedy struck again, and she lost her husband the following year. The double loss left her feeling incredibly lonely, as both Squirt and her husband had provided her with the love and companionship she needed in her life. Despite the immense pain she was going through, Carole remained strong and tried to focus on the beautiful memories she had shared with both of them.

Sonny.

The story of Sonny is a tale of feline companionship and miraculous occurrences. It is also a story about how Carole and I came to meet, so please excuse the length, but I am excited to share it with you.

In the beginning ... One day, my neighbor asked me to help her investigate something she had heard in a storage area under her house. She noticed that many things on a shelf in the storage area had been displaced, and she believed a raccoon or some other animal had gotten in there. I decided to go over and help her. As we entered the storage area, we had to crawl farther in. Using a flashlight, I shone it toward a corner under the house and immediately saw little eyes. I realized that it was a cat. We got out and left the doors open so that the cat could escape.

I decided to wait and take a video of the cat coming out. After a few minutes, I saw the cat come out the door and head toward the road in front of our houses. I thought the cat might be a female with kittens and was looking for help; it would walk a bit, stop, and look back as if to ensure I was following it. It walked underneath the deck in the back of my neighbor's house across the street and decided to lay down. I sat on the ground by the deck so the cat would feel more comfortable, and I waited for it to come over to me.

After about fifteen minutes and many phone pictures later, the cat came over toward me. It showed a small amount of reluctance at first when it started to rub against me, but it immediately allowed me to touch it. I tried to get as many pictures as I could so I could put it online and find out if it belonged to someone.

After bonding with it so it would trust me, I started back toward my house. The cat began to follow me, so I got some food together and put it out on the porch. It ate and stayed around, returning every day after that. The cat ended up staying around for over a month. During this time, I tried hard to find its original home, but nobody responded to the information I had put in the newspaper or on flyers and social media. So I decided to find it a new home.

My husband and I called the cat Sonny. It just seemed fitting for him. He was an orange tabby cat with the most loving eyes. Sitting and petting him, I noticed a beautiful, wavy look on his fur. I looked the fur type up online, and it resembled some of the characteristics of a Rex cat, which are known for their wavy and/or curly hair. It is possible that Sonny had inherited those traits from his feline relatives.

I worked for weeks putting up flyers everywhere and spreading the word to friends so that I could find Sonny a home. One day, I got a call from Anne, whom you now know as the owner of Kelly Clyde. Anne mentioned that she might know someone who would love to give the cat a home. She had seen the flyer I had posted at my local gym. I was so happy that someone had taken the time to care and help me in my efforts to find Sonny a forever home.

Sonny remained outside our house, near our front porch. He slept there, ate there, and hung out during the day. I spent a lot of time with Sonny on the porch. He would come over to me, jump on my lap, and want me to pet him or give him cat treats. I could not believe how affectionate and comfortable he had become with me and our home. I thought night and day about how to make Sonny part of our family of six cats and two dogs, but I had to be realistic. Our cats were older and settled. Bringing another older cat—who wanted a lot of attention and human contact—into the home would not be fair to him or my other animals, so I kept at it to find him a loving home.

After Sonny had been living with our outdoor cat family for almost a month, I received a call from a wonderful woman named Carole. She had been in contact with Anne about the possibility of adopting Sonny and was eager to meet him. Carole planned to come over and sit outside with me while we waited for Sonny to show himself. At first, he was reluctant to come close, but after several visits, he grew used to Carole's voice and scent. Eventually, Carole was ready to take Sonny home with her. Now, they are both very happy. Sonny loves to sleep and relax on the back of the couch in Carole's upstairs family room. He is always excited to see Carole when she comes home, and she loves hearing him coming down the stairs to greet her.

I am thankful for individuals like Carole and Anne. They not only helped me find a home for Sonny and gain great friends, but I have also become Sonny's Aunt Lori. Sometimes, I get to cat-sit Sonny when Carole is away. What a great exchange! Sonny is, indeed, a fortunate cat. Miracles do happen!

Gracie's Discovery of Feline Love

Tiger and Flower

Gracie has always had dogs in her life, but her perception changed once she started cat-sitting for me and my six house cats and outside feral cats. Her family, too, started appreciating the company of cats. Gracie's daughter was only three when she started accompanying her to feed and play with the cats. Though her daughter had never been around cats much before, she enjoyed being around them. She also loved pouring milk into their bowls and placing their food on their mats. This experience instilled in her the desire to have her own feline friend.

Gracie and her family are now proud owners of two adorable cats, Tiger and Flower. Tiger is a male, orange and white in color; while Flower is a female, gray and white in color, both being two years old. The story of how Gracie and her family found their cats is quite interesting. They were picking up something at a friend's house when they were told about a litter of kittens in a barn. The kittens had been born to a stray cat who had taken shelter in the barn. A young boy living on the farm had given the kittens lots of attention; thus, they were pretty tame. At the time, they were only six weeks old, and that's when Gracie's daughter fell in love with them. She cried the entire way home in the car for one of the kittens and did not stop begging the rest of the day. The next morning, Gracie and her husband decided to adopt one of the kittens, and as her daughter had fallen in love with the orange-and-white male first, they decided to bring his bobtailed sister, Flower, home as a playmate.

Tiger.

Flower.

Flower and Tiger are two cats with distinct personalities. Flower is a shy cat who likes to spend time alone, while Tiger is an attention-loving cat who enjoys being in the spotlight. They were both able to adapt to their new home and surroundings because Gracie and her family live on a large farm, and the cats are able to roam in the yard securely.

Both cats are excellent communicators. They know how to get what they want. When they need to go outside, they go to the door, and when they are hungry, they jump on the counter. They follow Gracie and her family around and meow when they want attention and love. Tiger and Flower also prefer to nap on Gracie and her family's beds instead of their own.

Gracie indicates that she "loves cuddling with her furry friends and listening to their soft purrs of contentment." She believes that waking up to their adorable meows is the perfect start to her day. Gracie's daughter also adores Tiger and Flower. She loves holding them like babies, dancing with them gently, and listening to music while they sit on her lap.

Rescuing the two kittens has had a profound impact on the family. They have become so attached to their cats that they now feel like they are a part of the family. The idea of waking up without hearing their soft meows or feeling their gentle touch while feeding them is unimaginable. Tiger and Flower have also developed a great rapport with Joy, the family's Australian shepherd. Watching them play together brings a lot of joy and laughter.

Sherry: A Real Cat Lady

The Wisconsin Farm Kitties, the Shop Kitties, the Southern Pines Farm Kitties, and the Cat Colonies

Sherry is a passionate cat lover who has taken care of over fifty cats in her lifetime. She is still caring for many felines, including feral ones. No matter where she lived or what she was doing, Sherry always had cats around her. This story will showcase some of the wonderful feline friends she has had throughout her life.

Sherry had always considered herself a dog person, but when she and her husband bought a beautiful farm in Wisconsin, she found herself falling in love with cats. The barn on the property was home to three cats named Butterscotch, Taffy, and Garfield. Sherry would often go into the barn to play with them and give them food. The cats were very friendly, despite having lived outside. Initially, Sherry's husband did not want them inside, but they soon became part of the family and moved inside.

Ultimately, Butterscotch, Taffy, and Garfield were joined on the farm by other kitties with names such as Clementine, Lincoln, and even Plutarch. They, too, enjoyed life around the farm, getting plenty of attention, love, and all the food they could feast their eyes on. By the time Sherry and her husband had eventually decided to move from Wisconsin to Southern Pines, North Carolina, at least ten cats were living on Sherry's farm and enjoying the wonderful life she was giving them. Because Butterscotch, Taffy, and Garfield had been there all their lives, Sherry felt it better that they stay at home. They were already spoiled by many of the neighboring farm folks, so she knew they would always be OK.

Precious.

The Southern Pines farm was also a beautiful place that Sherry and her husband purchased. Again, some of the cats were outside, and some were inside, but boy, did they have a lot of room to roam. After moving to Southern Pines, Sherry opened a shop in nearby downtown Pinehurst that offered women's clothing and other accessories. This was the first of two shops she would have. Shortly after she opened, she went to the vet and told them she was looking for a shop kitty to keep her company. Fortunately, they had just received a call from one of their clients who had indicated that they were about to put their ten-year-old cat down because they could not bring it with them on their move. Sherry was sad to hear that these people were about to do this, but she was also happy that she could provide it with a home and a fun place to roam. LC, or Lucky Cat, a gray tabby cat, got another chance to live, and Sherry got another companion. LC would sit on the back of a stuffed chair Sherry had in the shop. However, LC had seizures, and as she got older, they happened more often. She lived until the age of nineteen.

Rusty.

Sherry's second shop, which she opened in Southern Pines, had three cats named Isabella, Gracey, and Alley. Isabella was rescued from someone who was moving out of town. She was a calico cat and was older and would rest in her bed most of the time in the shop. There was also Grace, otherwise known as Amazing Grace, who was a gray cat that had been found roaming around downtown Pinehurst. And, lastly, there was Alley. Her name reflects where she lived, which was in the alley behind the Pinehurst shop. Alley was a black cat with beautiful, green eyes. She would roam around outside most of the day and would come in at night.

Fluffy.

The three cats got along great. Isabella and Grace had their beds in the front window of the shop, so they could see what was going on outside. Unfortunately, when Sherry decided to close down the Southern Pines shop, Isabella had already passed away. So Sherry took Alley to her house and Grace to the Pinehurst shop. Grace had a window seat in the bathroom that faced the street, and many customers came to talk to her through the window. Some of them even came just to see her. One woman, who often visited the shop with her husband, loved Grace so much that her husband would sit and talk to Grace while she shopped. Sadly, Grace died. However, as a tribute to her, the woman and her husband gave Sherry a portrait of Grace as a gift.

Sylvia.

Sherry has devoted a large part of her life to rescuing and helping cats, whether they are older or small kittens. She has given them a chance to live another day! Sherry is a person who loves cats to the extent that she can be considered a real-life cat lady! Below is the list of all Sherry's feline friends.

The Wisconsin Kitties: Butterscotch, Taffy, Garfield, Little Bit, Clancy, Clementine, Lincoln, Annie, Red, and Plutarch

The Shop Kitties: Grace, LC (Lucky Cat), Alley, and Isabella

The Southern Pines Farm Kitties: Zoe, Rosie, Rusty, Stanley, Miss Kittie, Sophia, Mizmo, Frieda, Bella, Oney, Twoey, Julius, Mommy, Louis, Tyke, Precious, Callie, Heidy, Fraidy, Sylvia, Benny, Little Bit, Sylvie, and Jude

The Cat Colonies: Pumpkin, Cry Baby, Little Black Kitty, Fluffy, Stripes, Blondie, Big Boy, Mr. Gray, Beauty, Pretty, Shadow, and Newby

(Sadly, while drafting this story, Sherry's longtime feline companion and her first rescue, Precious, passed away at the age of twenty-two. Precious was a black cat who enjoyed a long life with Sherry. She will be missed.)

Sandy's Scraggly Melba

Melba Toast

Melba (as a kitten).

Sandy and her husband, Jim, have always had dogs. They used to have at least two dogs at a time, and they had rescued all of them. However, Sandy had always wanted a kitten, but she knew that they would have to wait until they had both retired, so they could have enough time to spend with it. After retiring and moving from Michigan to North Carolina, Sandy and Jim settled into a new home and adopted a puppy named Fletcher. Sandy thought it was an excellent opportunity to get a kitten to keep Fletcher company. She and her husband had always opted for pet adoption to give animals a chance to lead long and healthy lives. So Sandy contacted the local chapter of Animal Advocates of the United States to find a kitten.

Sandy chose a young and tiny female kitten with wild-looking eyes. She looked a bit scruffy with her fur sticking up all over. When Sandy brought her home, Jim was surprised by the kitten's appearance and jokingly hinted that she looked like an owl. He knew that the kitten might not have been adopted because of her looks, so he told Sandy they had saved her just in time, because if they hadn't, "she would have been toast by tomorrow." As soon as the words came out of his mouth, he knew the kitten would be named Melba, as in Melba Toast.

Melba (as an adult).

When Melba was just a scraggly little kitten with unusual eyes, no one could have guessed how beautiful she would grow up to be. As she matured, she and Fletcher became close friends and lived happily together until Fletcher passed away in 2012. Melba's influence extended beyond her friendship with Fletcher, however. Sandy and Jim, who had never had a cat together before, fell in love with Melba and became lifelong dog and cat lovers thanks to her charming personality. Sandy and Jim were very sad, to say the least, when Melba passed away in 2014.

Mallory's Miracles at BlackJack Cottage

Annie, Abigail, and Mr. Kitty

This is a heartwarming story about Mallory and her beloved cats, who reside in a cozy home called BlackJack Cottage. Among her feline friends are two stunning calicos, named Annie and Abigail, as well as a delightful outdoor tabby mix named Mr. Kitty. Along with her loyal dog, Gracie, these four furry companions bring endless joy and love into Mallory's life and home.

Annie.

Annie, the elder of the two cats, is now eighteen years old and has been a part of Mallory's life since she was a tiny kitten. Mallory immediately fell in love with Annie's beautiful calico colors and her affectionate nature. Annie had been rescued after someone had left her in a cardboard box outside a veterinarian's office. Despite being eighteen years old, Annie still retains her youthful spirit and enjoys nothing more than curling up on the windowsill in Mallory's bedroom. From there, she can watch the birds and squirrels playing in the yard.

Abigail was the only kitten from her litter to survive a tragic accident where they were hit by a car. Without any hesitation, Mallory took her in and carefully nursed her back to good health. Since then, Abigail has become a lively and sometimes mischievous addition to BlackJack Cottage. She has a habit of stealing Annie's food when she isn't looking, and she loves it when her Auntie Lori takes care of them, because Lori always brings her treats. Abigail brings much joy and laughter to Mallory, and over the years, she has developed a special bond with Annie. They have become great companions, and their special bond warms Mallory's heart.

Abigail.

Mr. Kitty has been a beloved presence in the yard of BlackJack Cottage for over fourteen years. When he first showed up one day, Mallory noticed that he was already neutered, indicated by the clip on his ear. For several years, everyone assumed that Mr. Kitty was a female until Mallory saw him laying in the yard and realized that he was, in fact, a male. From that moment on, his name was changed to Mr. Kitty.

Mr. Kitty usually lives outside, but sometimes he comes into the foyer when the front door is open, and he meows for treats. However, he does not go any farther than the foyer. On many days, you can see him lying in the front yard, enjoying the sun and the peaceful landscape of Mallory's yard. He also loves Mallory's dog, Gracie, and he will sometimes follow Mallory as she walks Gracie around the neighborhood.

Mr. Kitty has the most beautiful eyes, and you can tell he is an old soul by his whitish beard and slow walk. His meow is very soft and low, and he shows affection with a little head-butt. Sometimes, he visits Auntie Lori's house for extra food. He sits patiently on the brick wall in her backyard, staring through the kitchen window, and he always gets what he wants.

Mr. Kitty.

Mallory takes immense pride in caring for her feline friends—Annie, Abigail, and Mr. Kitty. She ensures that they are provided with the best quality food, the coziest beds, and ample toys to keep them entertained. Every day, she showers them with love and affection, and her love for animals is truly remarkable. She dedicates her time and energy to helping animals in need, and she shares her resources with them whenever possible.

Char and Jim's Charming Cats

Maggie Rose, Sam, Beanie, and ET

Char and her husband, Jim, have loved animals for as long as they can remember. Over the years, they have provided a safe and loving home for many dogs and cats. Among their furry companions, they have had the pleasure of caring for a beautiful Himalayan named

Precious and several Persian cats, including Maggie Rose (Magnolia Rose), Sam, and Beanie. In addition to these feline friends, they rescued a gray cat named ET, who found them.

Beanie.

Jim was not always a cat person, but his perception changed when he and Char assisted a family member by adopting a Himalayan cat named Bobbie. Jim was smitten with the cat, and they eventually added a Himalayan cat to their family, naming it Precious. Later, when Char and Jim were moving to their current home, Jim gave Char a special basket for her birthday, and inside that basket was a white, three-month-old Persian kitten they named Maggie Rose. She quickly became a beloved member of their family.

Three years later, Char received another gift, a male beige-and-white Persian named Sam, from her nephew. After Sam passed away, Maggie Rose was left feeling quite lonely. Char and Jim decided to get her a brother, so they drove back to the breeder in Charlotte, North

Carolina, who'd had the last litter of Persians. From the litter, they chose Beanie, a male kitten who has since become their most beloved furry companion. Beanie is now fourteen years old and is still cherished by the family.

Beanie and Magnolia Rose became fast friends and were happy kitties together, until one day, Char and Jim were watching TV in their Carolina room, which opens on three sides with a full window, and they saw a kitten. They were puzzled that the kitten was in their courtyard because it was enclosed by a six-foot-high brick wall.

ET.

Char and Jim went outside, and the kitten was curled up near a wooden dog figurine in the back but did not run away when they tried to approach it. They decided to bring it inside, but Maggie Rose was not happy about it and she hissed at the kitten. They called the kitten ET but decided that she would need to stay outside in the courtyard. Jim and Char provided her with a small cat house and all the food and water she could eat. They also got ET neutered and implanted with a chip in case she went missing. Beanie loved to sit on the other side of the window, pawing with her. Maggie Rose, on the other hand, wanted nothing to do with the kitten.

Unfortunately, after eight months, one day, ET went over the courtyard wall and did not come back. Char and Jim offered a reward of two hundred dollars for her return, posted in the local newspaper, and posted on Facebook asking for ET to come home. Thankfully, their most welcoming call came a month after the day she'd left, and it was from the chip company giving them the number of where she was. Char and Jim called, and they were assured she was OK. She had been living in a neighborhood approximately ten blocks from their house, being fed by people in the neighborhood, and a cleaning lady in the neighborhood had noticed that ET had been bitten on the head. She immediately got her into her truck and took ET to a veterinarian. Char and Jim met the lady at the veterinarian's office, where they paid the bill for ET's care and gave the lady the reward.

While driving home with ET, Char and Jim decided she would no longer be an outside cat. They decided to keep her in their home office for a week. She was great with using the litter box, and Beanie slept all day and night next to the door.

After a week, Jim told Char it was time to open the door and see what would happen. Of course, Beanie was ecstatic. He had another friend to play with. Unfortunately, Maggie Rose continued to hiss at ET. She never bonded, even up until she passed away five years later, despite how badly ET tried to befriend her.

After Maggie Rose's passing, Jim sent pictures of Maggie Rose to a company that makes a stuffed animal that looks like your pet. ET would sit by it and softly paw at it. ET continues to love that stuffed Maggie Rose, which they occasionally move around the house. When people visit, they are surprised at how realistic it is, and ET apparently is, too.

Char and Jim firmly believe a rescued animal is appreciative, loving, and protective. They are now a family of two rescues—their dog, Rambo, and ET—and their adorable Persian, Beanie.

Carol's Story: A Love for Cats

Needles, Sambo, and Rusty

Carol's love of cats began in 1956 when she was just three years old. Unfortunately, she had become very sick with mumps, measles, chicken pox, and pneumonia, all within a six-week period. As a result, she had to stay in the hospital for almost six weeks.

Sambo.

When Carol was well enough to go home, she received visitors from her family church. Three ladies came to see her, each bringing a special gift. The first lady gave her a beautiful, small vase, while the second brought a little girl's purse that looked like a doll. However, the third lady had something very different in mind: she brought Carol a little male kitten.

Carol was thrilled to see the kitten, and the lady explained that this was a gift for Carol since she had been through so much with her illnesses, including measles. Since Carol was only three years old and could not pronounce many words, she thought the lady from her church had said the kitten's name was Needles, not the word *measles*. The name stuck with Carol. His name would be Needles, and he would become Carol's special companion and would help her through her recovery.

Years later, when Carol had children of her own, she adopted an all-black male kitten and named him Sambo. Sambo was a funny cat who loved to play with all of Carol's children, even participating in games of hide-and-seek. He seemed to understand what they were doing and would also hide and wait for the kids to try to find him. Carol and the kids thought he was part human because he was so smart and seemed to understand whatever was going on.

The kids loved to put a bib on Sambo and feed him in the high chair in the kitchen. Sambo would sit there and eat whatever they gave him. He enjoyed the attention and was very curious about what the kids were doing. One day, he even picked up a paintbrush in his teeth, and the brush end hit the paper as if Sambo were helping with the paint-by-numbers.

Sambo was also very protective of all the children, especially when Carol adopted her daughter, Jennifer, and brought her home from the hospital. Sambo would sleep in Jennifer's crib at the end of the bed and seemed to be her protector. He was always by her side until he passed away at the age of sixteen.

Carol and her family currently have a lovable orange tabby cat named Rusty. They adopted Rusty from an animal shelter when he was a kitten. Rusty has a huge appetite and often wakes Carol up at night wanting to be fed. Carol never minds getting up and giving Rusty a little snack.

Rusty.

Rusty is a very affectionate cat and loves to cuddle. He gets a bit sad when the family goes on trips. Whenever they start packing their bags, Rusty jumps inside the suitcase and even tries to hold it down while lying on top of it, as if he does not want them to leave him behind. He is a very important part of Carol's family and always will be.

My Life Lessons from Cats

Over the past twelve years, I have welcomed cats into my life and learned a great deal from them. Cats, both domestic and feral, have been a fundamental part of my life, teaching me valuable lessons along the way. As a devoted cat lover and caretaker of six house cats and a colony of feral cats, I have gained profound insights into life, relationships, and the nature of these creatures.

First and foremost, cats have taught me the importance of patience and understanding. Each cat has its own distinct personality, quirks, and preferences. Some are social and affectionate, while others are more independent. By observing and interacting with my cats, I have learned to respect their individuality, be patient in building trust, and foster bonds based on mutual respect.

Cats have also shown me the value of living in the present. Unlike humans, who sometimes dwell on the past or worry about the future, cats seem to live in the moment and revel in life's simple pleasures. By trying to be as carefree and relaxed as they are, I have become more mindful and appreciative of everyday life.

Caring for feral cats has deepened my compassion and empathy for all living beings. Feral cats face numerous challenges, and by providing food, shelter, and medical care to these vulnerable animals, I have witnessed the transformative power of compassion and the impact of small acts of kindness. It warms my heart.

In conclusion, my six house cats and the feral cats I care for have been my greatest teachers, sharing invaluable lessons on patience, boundaries, and compassion. Through their presence in my life, I have gained a deeper understanding of myself, my relationships with others, and the interconnectedness of all living beings. As I continue my journey with these beloved feline companions, I am grateful for the wisdom they impart and the joy they bring into my life each day. One of the most important lessons they have taught me is to find joy in the simple things in life, and to never take the many wonderful things around me for granted. The simple things in life are important.

Bibliography

Alaa Elassar, "National Black Cat Day: Here are Five Facts to Know About Our Black Feline Friends." *CNN*, October 27, 2019, https://www.cnn.com/2019/10/27/us/national-black-cat-day-trnd/index.html.

CatCon, "About Us," *Catcon Worldwide*, Accessed May 9, 2024, https://www.catconworldwide.com/about/.

Catherine Wehrey, "Hubble and Copernicus" *The Huntington*, November 8, 2012, https://huntington.org/verso/hubble-and-copernicus.

Clay Jenkins, "The Future of Declawing Cats: Will Vets Continue the Controversial Practice?" *Petshun*, May 6, 2024, https://petshun.com/article/will-vets-still-declaw-cats.

Elizabeth Brown Pryor, *Clara Barton: Professional Angel*. (University of Pennsylvania Press, 1987).

Emma Stenhouse, "All About Polydactyl Cats: The Cats With 'Mitten' Paws," *Rover*, December 14, 2023, https://www.rover.com/blog/polydactyl-cats/.

Erin McCarthy, "11 Facts About Hemingway's Cats," *Mental Floss*, July 10th, 2019, https://www.mentalfloss.com/article/587504/hemingways-cats-facts.

Hemingway Home. "Our Cats," *Hemingway Home*, Accessed May 1, 2024, https://www.hemingwayhome.com/our-cats.

Henri Troyat, *Catherine the Great*. (Boston Massachusettes: E.P. Dutton, 1980).

History.com Editors. "Florence Nightingale." *History.com*, April 24, 2023, https://www.history.com/topics/womens-history/florence-nightingale-1.

Joy Shiller, "Nightingale's Cats: The Nightingale Felines," *Country Joe McDonald*, Accessed May 29, 2024, https://www.countryjoe.com/nightingale/cats.htm.

Kat Eschner, "Mark Twain Liked Cats Better Than People," *Smithsonian Magazine*, October 16, 2017, https://www.smithsonianmag.com/smart-news/mark-twain-liked-cats-better-people-180965265/.

Kenneth E. Davison, "The Search for the Hayes Administration," *Rutherford B. Hayes Presidential Library and Museums*, Fall, 1978, https://www.rbhayes.org/research/hayes-historical-journal-hayes-administration/.

Kristi Finefield, "Coolidge's Cat: Out of the Bag!" *Library of Congress (blog)*, September 27, 2018, https://blogs.loc.gov/picturethis/2018/09/coolidges-cat-out-of-the-bag/.

Michele B. Snyder, "What Does a Cat Microchip Look Like?" *21 Cats*, Accessed May 9, 2024, https://www.21cats.org/what-does-a-cat-microchip-look-like/.

Patricia Barey and Therese Burson. *Julia's Cats: Julia Child's Life in the Company of Cats*. (New York, NY: Abrams Books, 2012).

Presidential Pet Museum, "Abraham Lincoln's Cats," *Presidential Pet Museum*, January 9, 2014, https://www.presidentialpetmuseum.com/pets/abraham-lincoln-cats/.

Presidential Pet Museum, "Theodore Roosevelt's Slippers," Accessed May 9, 2024, https://www.presidentialpetmuseum.com/theodore-roosevelts-slippers/.

Robert K. Massie, *Catherine the Great: Portrait of a Woman*. (New York, NY: Random House, 2011).

Sio Hornbuckle, "10 Iconic Women Who Prove 'Cat Lady' Is a Compliment." *Kinship*, January 16, 2024, https://www.kinship.co.uk/cat-lifestyle/iconic-cat-ladies.

Stephen B. Oates, *A Woman of Valor: Clara Barton and the Civil War*. (Free Press: May 1, 1995).

Virginia Rounding, *Catherine the Great: Love, Sex, and Power*. (Manhattan, NY: St. Martin's Press, 2006).

Printed in the United States
by Baker & Taylor Publisher Services